ORGANIZATIONS CONNECTED

Other titles in the
Systemic Thinking and Practice Series:
Work with Organizations
edited by David Campbell & Ros Draper
published and distributed by Karnac

Campbell, D. *Learning Consultation: A Systemic Framework*

Campbell, D. *The Socially Constructed Organization*

Campbell, D., Coldicott, T., & Kinsella, K. *Systemic Work with Organizations: A New Model for Managers and Change Agents*

Campbell, D., Draper, R., & Huffington, C. *A Systemic Approach to Consultation*

Campbell, D., & Grønbæk, M. *Taking Positions in the Organization*

Cooklin, A. *Changing Organizations: Clinicians as Agents of Change*

Haslebo, G., & Nielsen, K. S. *Systems and Meaning: Consulting in Organizations*

Huffington, C., & Brunning, H. (Eds.) *Internal Consultancy in the Public Sector: Case Studies*

McCaughan, N., & Palmer, B. *Systems Thinking for Harassed Managers*

Oliver, C. *Reflexive Inquiry: A Framework for Consultancy Practice*

Credit Card orders, Tel: +44(0) 20-7431-1075; Fax: +44(0) 20-7435-9076
Email: shop@karnacbooks.com

ORGANIZATIONS CONNECTED

A Handbook of Systemic Consultation

Edited by

David Campbell & Clare Huffington

Systemic Thinking and Practice Series:
Work with Organizations

Series Editors
David Campbell & Ros Draper

KARNAC

First published in 2008 by
Karnac Books
118 Finchley Road
London NW3 5HT

British Library Cataloguing in Publication Data

A C.I.P. for this book is available from the British Library

ISBN: 978–1–85575–669–4

Edited, designed, and produced by Communication Crafts

Printed in Great Britain

www.karnacbooks.com

CONTENTS

SERIES EDITORS' FOREWORD

In this Series, we have always sought to offer professionals contemporary, relevant, and novel ways of developing their practice. We believe that this book continues that tradition, demonstrating again through the variety and richness of the contributors' descriptions of their experiences as organizational consultants the relevance of systemic ideas to both the complexity of twenty-first-century organizational structures and life and the daily demands and dilemmas faced by managers and consultants.

David Campbell and Clare Huffington are both pioneering organizational consultants with many years' experience of finding innovative and convincing ways to offer systemic ideas and practices to the corporate world in the public, private, and voluntary sectors.

Describing and charting the way in which a consultant working from the systemic paradigm brings a unique lens to the understanding of organizational complexity has been, and remains, a challenging task in a global corporate world where the demand is always for products, new interventions, and approaches that "work" and can be measured.

The structure of the chapters in this book offers readers the opportunity to connect to each contributor's account of his or her work, showing how systemic ideas and practices shape a piece of consultation while simultaneously respecting the need for the generic stages of consultation identified by the editors in their Introduction to remain visible and recognizable to the readers, whatever familiarity and fluency with systemic thinking practices they may bring to the text.

The interventions described by the contributors, all established and respected consultants, elegantly reflect a number of facets of the value of systemic work in organizations—namely, the distinctive ways systemic practitioners pay attention to and use feedback, examine and seek to understand beliefs that sustain repetitive patterns of behaviour, explore the development over time of cultural values in an organization, seek to increase possible explanations for the above, and clarify roles and tasks in relation to specific contexts, to mention only a few.

This book clearly shows the underlying thinking of experienced consultants deciding how to position themselves in organizations, creating networks of relationships around a variety of tasks over time, seeking to enable organizational change to occur, and redefining their relationships with their clients over time and according to organizational need using a systemic lens. That this is clear is itself an important contribution to developments in the field this Series aims to reflect.

The traditional definition of a "handbook" is: a manual or small reference book providing specific information or "how-to-do-it" instruction about a subject. The subtitle of this book—*A Handbook of Systemic Consultation*—might not sit comfortably in the minds of systemic purists, but because of the helpful presentation of a rich array of systemic ideas, and a sequential format for conducting consultations, we think the title aptly reflects the content of the book.

We believe that this book is a timely addition to the literature in the field and hope the reader's appetite is whetted and she or he feels more equipped to try some of these ideas for her/himself.

David Campbell
Ros Draper
London, 2008

ABOUT THE EDITORS AND CONTRIBUTORS

Philip Boxer has consulted on strategy since the beginning of the 1980s, supporting both individuals and leadership teams across many different industry sectors, both public and private, to bring about transformational change. His chapter with Carole Eigen has emerged from their shared interest in the leadership challenges that organizations face from asymmetric forms of demand, to which he brings his focus on the identification and mitigation of risks associated with failing to develop requisite agility (www.asymmetricdesign.com). He is currently on the staff of the Software Engineering Institute at Carnegie Mellon University, Pittsburgh, USA, where he is developing the methods associated with working with software systems-intensive organizations. (p.boxer@brl.com)

David Campbell is a consultant clinical psychologist based at the Tavistock Clinic in London. In addition to a clinical practice, he has developed training courses in supervision, professional doctorate research, and Master's-level family therapy training. He has established a long-standing international practice as a management and leadership trainer and organizational consultant specializing in applying systemic models to strategic planning and team-building work with teams, services, and small organizations in both the private and public sector, including health, education, social services, and the voluntary sector. He offers role consultation, supervision, and executive coaching. He has written extensively about consultation, including his recent *Taking Positions in the Organization* (Campbell & Grønbæk, 2006) and is the co-editor of the Systemic Thinking and Practice Series. (david@campbell340 .freeserve.co.uk)

Carole Eigen is Principal at Bridgewater Psychological Associates, Bridgewater, New Jersey, USA. She is an experienced clinical psychologist, university educator, and family systems supervisor. She designs and implements learning systems to support leaders who must re examine their personal/professional role in order to engage in transformational agendas. She utilizes psychoanalytic, systemic, and group relations methodology to facilitate a reflexive consultation process for managers and organizational consultants who work in complex systems that are in transition. (ceigen@optonline.com)

Myrna Gower is a systemic psychotherapist with many years' experience in private clinical practice, teaching, and organizational consultancy. Her interest and experience in individual consultation to strategic management and deal negotiation initiated an invitation to join Bright Side Productions, a coaching consultancy, in 1999. She has a special interest in training and the development of leadership initiatives and has a long association as trainer and clinical supervisor with the Tavistock Clinic, Prudence Skynner Family Therapy Clinic, and Royal Holloway, University of London. She remains involved with the accreditation of training courses in family therapy as well as the registration of clinical practitioners and supervisors through the Association for Family Therapy. She has published in the area of training and clinical practice and is currently conducting doctoral research. (myrna@gower.me.uk) (www.brightsideoflife .co.uk)

Marianne Grønbæk trained as a social worker and as a systemic therapist, consultant, and supervisor. She is the chief consultant in MG-UDVIKLING, a small consulting firm based in Denmark and known for qualitative systemic thinking and practice. In addition to her work as a consultant, she does organizational and professional training in private and public organizations in Denmark, the United Kingdom, and Scandinavia. (mgn@dirker.dk)

Rita Harris is a consultant clinical psychologist and systemic psychotherapist. She is currently Clinical Director of the Child and Family Directorate and CAMHS Lead for the Tavistock Clinic in London. She has developed multi-agency services in partnership with local authorities for the most vulnerable children, young people, and their families. She also has extensive experience in developing, managing, and consulting to a range of services for children and young people and has a special interest in training and consulting to managers in the public sector. (rharris@ tavi-port.nhs.uk)

Clare Huffington is a freelance organizational consultant and executive coach and was, until early 2007, the Director of the Tavistock Consultancy Service in London. She is a clinical psychologist and worked as an educational psychologist, university lecturer, clinical psychologist, and family therapist before beginning to work with larger systems as an organizational consultant. Her main interest is in extending and developing the conceptual frame of reference used by organizational consultants to address the new challenges that organizations face in the twenty-first century. (clare.huffington@tiscali.co.uk)

Keith Kinsella is a Fellow of the Centre for Leadership Studies at Exeter University, where he coaches mature students on the e-learning MA in Leadership Studies. He also designs and facilitates situated and "emergent" development processes for executive teams, action inquiry sets, and partnership networks—as they grapple with dilemmas of change and continuity—seeking to exploit sources of tacit knowledge, encourage improvisation, and embody learning in everyday practice. To further his interest in processes that support development in real time ("close learning"), he is researching context-based action inquiry methods that foster the two-way interchange of knowledge between "academy" and "field", on the PhD programme at the Centre for Action Research in Professional Practice, Bath University. (kckinsella@btinternet.com)

Georgina Noakes set up the coaching consultancy Bright Side Productions in 1997 to work as an executive coach, teacher, and facilitator with senior executives in the corporate sector, at Board level, and in the professional services arena with leaders and their teams. She is a facilitator and chair for Windsor Leadership Trust and is on the faculty of the Adair Leadership Foundation. She is a member of the European Mentoring & Coaching Council and the Association for Coaching. She is one of the first executive coaches in the United Kingdom to have obtained an MSc in Coaching & Development (2005). Her research explored the influence of coaching conversations on the change process in legal practices. Her current interests are in relation to developing the interior landscape, narratives, and behaviour of leaders. She works with business partner Myrna Gower to create and deliver leadership interventions in organizational life. She is married to Richard, has two stepsons, and lives in Hampshire with a menagerie of animals. (georgina@brightsideoflife.co.uk) (www.brightsideoflife .co.uk)

Christine Oliver is Senior Lecturer in the School of Business and Management, Queen Mary, University of London; course leader for the MSc in Systemic Management, Coaching and Consultation for the Institute of Family Therapy; course leader for the MSc in Systemic Psychotherapy at Kensington Consultation Centre, London; and a consultant family therapist in the Department of Psychotherapy, St. Bartholomew's Hospital, London. She provides training and consultancy for a number of organizations in the United Kingdom, as well as working internationally. A primary interest is in consultancy methodologies for structuring dialogue to engender reflexive consciousness and practice in the workplace. She is co-author of *Complexity, Relationships and Strange Loops: A*

Reflexive Practice Guide (2003) and author of *Reflexive Inquiry* (2005). (oliver@madeleybarnes.u-net.com)

Simon Western is Founder/Director of Privileged Conversations Ltd., a consulting company that designs and delivers bespoke and imaginative leadership and coaching interventions. He has worked with a diverse range of CEOs and senior-level leaders in FTSE 100 and public sector companies. As an academic, he has taught leadership in executive education at McGill University, Bangalore Institute of Management, and Lancaster University. Until recently he was Director of Coaching at Lancaster University Management School. Previously he worked as a nurse, family therapist, clinical manager, and organizational consultant in the public sector. His current research and work interests are to design leadership and coaching interventions that focus on creativity and leadership spirit. His recent publication, *Leadership: A Critical Text* (2008), develops the concept of Leadership Formation (drawing on the monastic tradition of spiritual formation), which challenges conventional leadership development. He is a practising Quaker, and this has a strong influence on his work. (simonwestern@gmail.com) (www.simonwestern.com)

ORGANIZATIONS CONNECTED

Introduction

Six stages of systemic consultation

David Campbell & Clare Huffington

The strength—and the weakness—of the systemic model is that it provides the means for a continual search for meaning. It builds a picture of the ways parts of a whole are connected and speculates about possible meanings attributed to these patterns. Once a meaning is identified, however, a systemic observer must step back to acknowledge that, in identifying that particular meaning, he or she has created a new context and new possible meanings. And where does it all end?

For the purpose of working as a consultant or manager within an organization, a punctuation point has to be reached in order that a decision can be taken, a change made, or a problem resolved. At that point, a particular set of meanings will be used as a basis for action.

The strength of the model lies in its ability to identify many possible meanings from which to construct an understanding of what is going on, and then how best to intervene; its weakness is that it does not encourage people to develop a model of the world from one position. Thus, one could get caught in continually generating new meanings and not taking action when needed. The consultant working within a systemic framework is trying to help the client reach a position of having the minimum sufficient meanings to be able to move forward in a new way.

The systemic paradigm is based on the idea that, when we observe connectedness, we can see a pattern, and meaning arises from the interpretations we place on the pattern. Pattern leads to meanings. We find that clients in organizations have often got stuck with one particular meaning they are placing on events and that this is not allowing them to develop as individuals, as groups, or as a whole organization. Finding new meanings can loosen connections to a particular set of ideas that are producing the stuckness. It can do the equivalent of throwing open the windows of the sickroom to allow in light and air. Once new ideas and feedback are present, they generate further meanings and creativity is released in the organization, which enables people to solve their own problems.

In this introduction, we present generic ideas that we find essential in carrying out a piece of consultation from start to finish, and we explain the systemic thinking that can be applied at each stage, making reference to our own experiences or to those of the other contributors to this book. We also refer to techniques and ways of working with clients inspired by systemic thinking and used by us or our contributors in this work. We hope that in doing this, readers will be able to find tools and techniques they can use themselves in their own work as consultants or managers.

We asked each contributor to describe the way they use the systemic model in their consultancy practice and to begin their chapter by addressing the question: "What specific interpretation or application of systemic thinking will be underpinning the work in your chapter?" We wanted them to set out the key ideas that they would then illustrate via a case example or examples, where possible including detailed accounts of the exercises and techniques they use inspired by systemic thinking. We also asked them to conclude with an evaluation of the work, pinpointing its strengths and weaknesses and what the contributor learned from it as well as how it might be developed or applied in other situations.

The consultation process can be described in terms of six stages that we have identified as discrete and essential parts of a process consultation. The description of stages differs from other process consultation approaches (e.g., Shein, 1969; Schön, 1983) in:

» the emphasis on generating meaning at every stage of the process
» close collaboration with clients as co-creators of new meanings
» the relative backgrounding of the consultant and foregrounding of client leadership and action in producing change.

The six stages we are proposing are:

1. developing an understanding of the consultant's relationship to the client;
2. identifying a problem and making a contract for work;
3. designing a consultation;
4. working directly with the participants;
5. using continuous feedback;
6. evaluation.

1. Developing an understanding of the consultant's relationship to the client

Consultants are contacted for many reasons. The consultation has to be supported, and paid for, by someone or some group with sufficient authority to sanction the time, effort, and money involved. So the first question the consultant asks is, "What does consultation mean to this person, this group, or this organization?" The sponsor has been engaged in some internal debate among several points of view about how to manage change in the organization, represented by "the staff need some new input to help them through a difficult area", on the one hand, and "we don't want to make things worse by stirring things up with the staff", on the other. It may be that a particular individual sees him/herself as losing out in some way in the situation the organization is in and is seeking to bolster his or her position by securing external help (Selvini Palazzoli, 1986).

This makes us think hard about why the sponsor comes down on the side of bringing you in to consult to the organization. We find it helpful to imagine the discussion that took place in the organization that led to the final decision to contact a consultant. Was there heated debate . . . unanimity . . . agreement with conditions . . . or sulking acceptance, and what kind of reception might the consultant receive when he or she arrives to meet the clients? And why have you, in particular, been invited? Most commonly, the consultant has been chosen by word of mouth, personal recommendation, or some form of tendering process. Sponsors have had time to assess directly or indirectly whether you are both safe and effective for the organization. They will have some sense of whether their organization needs minor tweaking or wholesale change, and you are part of their expectation.

For example, in the chapter contributed by Simon Western, who is based at the Leadership Centre at Lancaster University, he describes how he was initially contacted by his client, the Chief Executive of the Centre for Excellence in Leadership in the Further Education and Learning and Skills Sector in the United Kingdom. She asked him to become her "personal leadership coach" at a time when she was facing a challenge to her leadership style. While successful as a leader of a further education college, her new task was to lead a partnership organization where she felt her existing style would not work. She may have hoped and expected that Western, from a centre of perhaps even greater leadership excellence in the university sector, would be able to help her be a better and different leader in a new context. Western goes on in his chapter to show how his client discovered that her task would not be to be more powerful or dominant but to construe leadership of a partnership of organizations in quite a different way from leadership of a single institution. He illustrates well the way the consultant working with a systemic model can generate new meanings that transform the initial request and expectations into a collaborative search for new meanings.

We have written elsewhere about the differences between the internal and external consultant, and these distinctions are also important at this stage of the process (Campbell, Draper, & Huffington, 1991; Huffington & Brunning, 1994). While the internal consultant may be seen to be safer, quicker to grasp the issues, and easier to confide in, the risk is that he or she will be seen as having a position and is therefore easier to disqualify—"She *would* say that!" We can see, for example, in the second case presented by Clare Huffington in her chapter, that the Human Resources (HR) Director in the IT company was keen to act on the recommendations from an external consultant that the organization needed to launch a leadership development intervention, especially for the top team and Chief Executive (CEO), both as individuals and as a group. However, the CEO had rejected this external advice as he did not consider it a key priority at the time.

It may have been too far from what was important for him or not linked in his mind with what were his priorities (perhaps a failure on the part of the external consultant to make that link effectively). So he turned to the HR Director—his internal consultant, if you like—for a different way to take forward the need for development. Her approach was more subtle, using coaching from a number of external providers in a stepwise process monitored by her, which the coaches called a "seeping model". This meant a gradual soaking in of new ideas over time. Although it took about 18 months, it did produce the result that the external consultant had originally advocated. This time, however, the intervention was able to integrate with the key priorities in the organization from the perspective of the CEO and other key stakeholders at all levels of the organization. This is because it became embedded in many layers of meaning.

We would say it is essential that the consultant working within a systemic framework pays attention to the question of ownership of the ideas that get generated. If they are not well rooted in the organization's experience and fundamentally linked to its key drivers, they will be rejected as too distant, external, or "foreign". This work is not about the consultant developing clever ideas but helping the clients to find, or re-find, their own meanings, cleverness, and creativity. The challenge for the consultant is to get close enough to really engage with the way the clients think while retaining sufficient distance to be able to comment on these thoughts and the way they are expressed so that the client notices this too.

2.   *Identifying a problem and making a contract for work*

We have frequently had experiences in which an organization presents a vague idea that something isn't right and something needs fixing, but they may not have any clearer notion of what needs attention. The clients will, nevertheless, want some clarity about the contract for work they are agreeing to (for a thorough and engaging discussion of the contracting phase, we would refer readers to Peter Block's *Flawless Consulting*, 1981); yet the systemic consultant will want to join the organization in such a way as to be able to observe the organizational process going on around him or her, and to have enough freedom and manoeuvrability to make some formulations about the meaning of the process to the organization. In this second stage, the consultant is trying to strike a balance between agreeing on a focus for the consultation and also leaving the focus broad enough to be able to see the organization in new ways as he or she interacts with it. This "balancing position" can be usefully discussed and negotiated with commissioning clients at the outset of the work.

Philip Boxer and Carole Eigen in their chapter describe how the reflexive consultation process that they designed enabled the CEO of a religious membership organization to take up a position from which he could question the model within which he himself was working as a leader. In the original meeting with the CEO, it had been agreed that an external consultant would certainly not know better than he how to meet the challenge of how to lead the organization in the future. The consultation process would have to be one that enabled the CEO himself to work out how to meet the challenge on behalf of the organization. Therefore Boxer and Eigen formed an internal "shadow consultation group" of four individuals working on contract or within the client system. This group was to work with the CEO and with Boxer as facilitator and Eigen as his shadow consultant. The goal of the facilitation was "to enable the group to notice what was being avoided or was difficult to surface in its own dynamics as it struggled with its task". The consultation process proceeded through monthly face-to-face meetings through three phases, the timing of which were determined by the emergent learning of the CEO and the consultation group; in other words, it was based on the internal logic of the consultation process and layers of meaning as they were uncovered. The final phase enabled the CEO to challenge a previously unquestioned assumption in the organization that was fundamental to its future and also to his leadership.

This example emphasizes that there are no "off-the-shelf" ways of working within the systemic model. Each consultation is tailored to the needs of the client, and the position the consultant(s) take up in the process must serve these needs effectively. In this case, the autonomy of the client needed to be respected, and the nature of the working group and the stages of the consultation were entirely driven by the development of his thinking about his role. We see consultation as an ongoing process that is triggered by the consultant's first contact but is continually evolving as the consultant and the organization interact around the consultation project.

3.   Designing a consultation

A crucial polarity for consultants is between the observing/reflecting position and the need to "put down a marker and act". This third stage requires the consultant to offer something specific, such as an explanation, a proposal, a policy, or a new structure. The ways this process can develop are varied, and one clear example of work in this stage is provided, in their chapter, by Georgina Noakes and Myrna Gower. Georgina Noakes had a long-standing relationship with the Human Resources department of a large legal firm, through which she frequently met to discuss ways to improve communication within the firm. The firm commissioned her to design and analyse a survey for the staff about communication. This revealed that the legal assistants wanted more feedback about what they were meant to be doing and how their work fitted in to the larger picture. This then prompted the senior partners to approach Noakes to remedy this situation, and she negotiated, with the partners and Gower, to design a structured leadership course for partners as a vehicle for improving the communication between the partners and their assistants.

Keith Kinsella, in his chapter, also provides a good example of the programme he designed to support the improvement of leadership in a local strategic partnership (LSP), a new type of organization set up by the UK government to re-focus the delivery of services to meet local community needs. The LSP includes police, the local health trust, education, voluntary, business, and other sectors. He had to find ways to support leadership development in a large and diverse group of busy people who wore several hats. His first idea had been to design a free-standing development programme that delegates would attend separately from their ongoing work together. But this proved impossible because of the pressure of time and competing priorities. What evolved instead was a way of working in real time with the LSP in their existing meetings but using what he calls a "close learning 'development sandwich'" or "layered approach to developing while doing". This involved simultaneously working at *intention* or purpose (both of learning and doing); at the *context(s)* for the work (many, including each constituent organizational context as well as the shared context); at *process,* so as to look at the emergent ways they were working together and how they could become more creative, and less formal and bureaucratic; and at *content,* the central strategic issues they needed to resolve together.

Thus, what he calls the performing process was shadowed all the way by the development perspective, with one or the other being brought to the foreground where appropriate. This was a powerful and effective process that quickly produced both concrete results and a creative and energized working process for the LSP. Kinsella comments that it was a very intense and demanding way of working for the consultant because of the need to be thinking at all the levels at once and needing to be quick on your feet and good at working in the moment. This is also an important feature of this approach, as we will see in more detail in Stage 5.

4.   Working directly with the participants

The way systemic consultants work with clients is experienced as quite different from the way other consultants work. Clients will typically say things like, "I never thought about our situation that way before"; "It is such a relief to be able to talk about what is really going on in our team in a safe way"; "I realize I don't have to come up with all the answers by myself—I can do what I do with you (consultant) with my colleagues now". They experience the intensity and depth of the approach in contrast to other approaches. One of the features of the style is of a real focus on meaning but without this being centred on the consultant. What is on the table is a shared exploration of the system from an inside and outside perspective—from the consultant who is outside looking in and the clients who are inside looking out—as well as their perspectives on each other's views

It can sometimes be difficult for clients to free themselves from the perspectives and meanings they already have. It is a common experience for a consultant working with a group to have members of that group using it as an opportunity to "sound off" their well-honed views without listening to one another at all. The consultant has to be able to develop tools and techniques to:

» help clients to think more systemically and less individually

» shift their well-worn patterns of thinking and interacting

» allow them to play and be creative

» create a context for them to come up with new ideas and new ways of behaving.

One way that clients begin to think systemically during the consultation is by the consultant asking "systemic questions" that invite the client to explore the way behaviour and ideas influence diverse parts of the organization. For example, rather than asking how someone tried to tackle a particular problem, a systemic question might ask: "When you tried to tackle the problem in that way, what effect did you notice on another department?", or "What have you observed in other parts of the organization that influenced you to try this approach?" Although the differences between these questions may appear slight, we find that when asked repeatedly over the course of a consultation, they do have the effect of helping people think more systemically about their behaviour.

There are many examples of how our contributors enable participants to generate new ideas in their work—for example, Keith Kinsella and his simple but effective use of Post-it Notes and working in smaller groups so everyone could have their say; using simple voting processes ("put your 3 red dots on the ideas you want to concentrate on"); and taking regular time-outs to take the group temperature. These techniques had the effect of constraining the usual formal meeting patterns and encouraging risk-taking and informality so that people could share ideas more quickly and easily and tackle some quite complex issues without the anticipated difficulty.

In his chapter, David Campbell takes a different approach in his consultation work by facilitating direct, dialogical communication among participants. In order to do this, he takes the statements people make about their work, identifies them as "position statements", and then places the position on a polarity line with other position statements. This has the effect of encouraging participants to talk to each other from different positions and thereby get more interested in ideas other than their own. For example, in one consultation a participant said their difficulty was that "there was no compassion from the kids to the carers"; Campbell turned this statement into a position—that clients show compassion for themselves, not others—and then contrasted that with the position at the other end of the polarity—that clients show compassion for others, not themselves. The staff group could then discuss why it may be important for clients to shift their positions in relation to the staff depending on what else was going on in their lives.

5.   Using continuous feedback

There is sometimes the sense in other descriptions of process consultation that it is enough to carefully diagnose the presenting problem or issue, design a consultation, and then sit back and let it roll! The difference between this approach and the systemic model we are describing here is the intensity of the work done in the moment. There is a need for the consultant to be alert at all times to opportunities to spot emerging patterns and to find ways to make these evident and usable to the client group so that they can become the basis for new meanings to be shared. In this sense it is an emergent, not prescriptive, process. Christine Oliver, in her chapter, identifies particular pieces of feedback as "moments of significance", and she describes the way she uses these moments to focus everyone's attention on a new way of understanding the process the group is going through. For example, she uses a poignant example of someone who, in the midst of the consultation work, sat in a chair, and it collapsed. The next day, the person reported that no one had phoned to see how she was, and she suggested that the group was not caring. Oliver used this event as feedback that touched on another important theme for the group—namely, the ambiguity of accountability in the organization, which meant that colleagues did not know who they could count on. She actively blocked further discussion about whether this was a caring group and led the group into discussion about this theme of accountability.

Another example of using ongoing feedback is represented in the chapter by Marianne Grønbæk. She uses the semantic polarities model with groups experiencing difficulties as a framework for "harvesting" the feedback from one phase of a consultation to lead into the next. Semantic polarities are the range of positions we may take within a particular theme or discourse in order to create meaning in a relationship with other positions. The use of a particular polarity emerges from an initial discussion on a topic with a group. For example, managers in a school staff group identified several themes in the difficulties they were experiencing in their meetings: cultural differences; authority levels; equality issues; responsibility; the need for rules. Grønbæk then describes how she created clarity and focus in the next phase of the discussion by suggesting that there might be a semantic polarity between, on the one hand, "rules and tools will create the best meetings and decisions" and, on the other, "being aware of your own and others' positions creates the best meetings and decisions". She then invited everyone to take positions in relation to their agreement with these polarities so as to create a conversation that would allow differences to be expressed in the group. The ensuing differences could then be teased out to allow more discussions based on further emerging polarities so as to finally allow decisions to be made about how future meetings of the staff group would be run. This example elegantly shows how, in stepwise fashion, using semantic polarities, differences can safely be expressed and used as a basis for expanding meaning in a group rather, than leading to insoluble conflict.

6. Evaluation

The consultant working within the systemic model would not usually see evaluation exclusively as a discrete stage in the consultation process but as a mindset throughout the work. The consultant is continually looking for pattern and meaning and trying to create a context for meanings to be examined and evaluated by clients as a basis for new decision-making and action. He or she is aiming to set off a whole series of learning cycles like fireworks all the time if possible (Kolb, 1984). However, the final test of the pudding is in the eating: it is not enough to generate lots of interesting meanings if it does not result in change that is linked to the original reason for calling in a consultant in the first place.

Of course, it is sometimes difficult to measure success against the original goals of the work because the goals can change based on the more developed analysis of the underlying issues that is part of the consultation process. And unexpected and surprising leaps forward can take place! But the consultant needs to be able to track these as time goes on. Nevertheless, there are various ways consultants have tried to pin down and isolate aspects of this organizational process in order to make more evidence-based judgements about what has happened and how the consultant might go forward.

As discussed above, the evaluation that Noakes and Gower describe resulted from a long-standing client interest in communication in the law firm. Interestingly, this evaluation revealed some dissatisfaction that led directly to the longer-term leadership training programme.

David Campbell and Marianne Grønbæk produced a previous volume about their work with positioning and semantic polarities (Campbell & Grønbæk, 2006), and for that publication they commissioned a researcher to interview three directors who had used this model of consultation in their own organizations. This allowed the authors to learn, from a more neutral source, about the outcome of their work, but also about some specific interventions that the participants found helpful.

Simon Western reports impressive data relating to the success of the partnership working of the Centre for Excellence in Leadership (CEL) following his work with the CEO and constituent organizations. For example, 96% of participants rated CEL programmes as good or very good; CEL worked with 91% of organizations in the further-education sector in the United Kingdom; and within the organization, leadership was distributed and internal communication improved.

Many of the learning points to emerge from Rita Harris's chapter are the result of a training course she established at the Tavistock Clinic. Members of the course, all of whom are managing services, are asked to bring their own work dilemmas to the course seminars, where they are discussed and evaluated by the group consisting of course members. Thus, over time, it becomes clear which interventions are having which impact within their services. This is an excellent method for evaluating ongoing work, but also, by placing the work in a course structure, the students/managers have the opportunity to receive ongoing supervision that allows them to step back and evaluate their own position in the system. Harris used these course discussions to develop her own learning about the impact of the systemic model. For example, she notes that service managers have reported reduced personal anxiety for every small problematic event, and that understanding the interconnectedness of systems has enabled them to make more sense of the emotional environment in their organizations.

Conclusion

In this introduction, we have tried to emphasize that it is important to see systemic consultation as both similar to and different from any other approach to consultation. Consultants from any walk of life would probably agree that these six stages of consultation are fundamental to the work, although they might cast them in different terms. But we have also highlighted some of the specific systemic concepts that make this approach radically different from many others, such as the careful attention to feedback during the consultation, the emphasis on interaction and dialogue, the appreciation that meaning arises from context, and the consultant seeing him/herself as part of what he or she observes. The chapters that follow go much further in elucidating these concepts and how they are put into the practice of work with organizations.

CHAPTER ONE

The system in the room:
the extent to which coaching
can change the organization

Clare Huffington

Commentary

In this chapter, Clare Huffington looks at the huge growth in the coaching market in organizations in all sectors in relation to the relative decline in the market for large-scale organizational consultancy and asks why this should be the case. Her particular question is whether one-to-one work is taking the place of consultancy to the system as a whole and the extent to which coaching is equal to achieving this task in an alternative form. The chapter draws attention to the retreat from the whole-systems thinking of the last ten years or so while emphasizing that many of the things organizations now want and need to do (partnership working, strategic alliances, mergers, and acquisitions) require the ability to work within and across systems.

After outlining the key ideas and techniques she uses in her work with coaching clients, Huffington explores via two case examples the extent to which it is possible to influence the organization as a whole via working with an individual client. In the first example, of work with a senior manager in an investment bank, it was possible to help the client to develop her systemic thinking to the extent that she herself took action to influence her colleagues and other senior leaders in the organization so that change took place. In the second example of work with senior leadership team members and subsequently the CEO of an IT company, individual work with a group of leaders built a critical mass of curiosity and desire for change in the system from the levels below the CEO that he eventually could not ignore.

One of the key questions that remains is whether coaching individuals in an organization can ever be more than the sum of the parts: the challenge to systemic practitioners may be to design new methods and approaches to changing whole systems that appeal to leaders in organizations today. A number of the subsequent chapters in this book illustrate some possible examples. [Eds.]

In a way, the title of this chapter is a bit odd. How could an individual approach to personal and professional development like coaching change an organization? On the other hand, why has there been such a massive growth in the coaching market in the last ten or so years, with organizations the major purchasers of the service for their senior executives. What do they see in it?

On one level, one could view this as an attempt by organizations to recruit and retain good people by offering personal development as an executive "perk"—I recently saw the provision of coaching described in a job advertisement as one of the benefits of becoming a manager at a large chain of retail stores. Or, on another level, people now seem to lack trust that organizations will look after them and support their development, given the vicious downsizing and redundancies of recent years. The support function is now outsourced to the burgeoning band of external coaches rather than to internal managers. This may be why individuals seek coaching for themselves even if their organizations do not offer it to them.

However, there is another possibility: that coaching is, as described by one of my clients, "the new organizational consultancy", a discrete, relatively cheap, controllable form of organizational consultancy compared with the large-scale major change consultancy popular in the 1980s and 1990s. There may be additional benefits from coaching. It mirrors or even simulates the kind of leadership organizations now need—that is, the leader as coach or facilitator rather than army general or bureaucrat. So the leader, by having coaching, learns vicariously how to coach the system. One might equally say that the manager learns how to coach individuals by being coached him/herself (Bell & Huffington, 2008).

Coaching could become a vehicle for change in an organization if it is offered to the chief executive or boss of the organization and/or the key decision-makers; and in this situation, for this idea to hold water, there would also need to be a critical mass of decision-makers who share the thinking derived from their use of coaching. My experience suggests that it is also possible that coaching offered to people at lower levels in the organization can awaken them to making different demands of those senior to them. This, in turn, can allow different conversations to take place at that level, leading to changes in the way the organization as a whole is led and in its future direction. The coaching would need to be of a particular kind from someone who sees him/herself as an "organization coach" as well as a personal developer (De Haan & Burger, 2005). It would not be the kind of coaching that seeks to turn the individual away from the organization but one that helps the individual face into it and deal more effectively with his or her role in it. It would need to be focused on the uncertain but creative boundary between the individual in the organization and "the organization in the individual" (Huffington, 2006). This means the feelings, thoughts, and beliefs held in the organization that become part of the individual as a result of his or her engagement with it.

I describe below how these ideas have evolved from the systemic framework.

The coach, the coachee, and the organization

The classic triangle of person, role, and system (Figure 1.1) describes how the individual derives relatedness and authority through his or her role in the system/organization (Miller & Rice, 1967a). This model helps the organizational consultant or manager to remember the mediating function of a person's role in relation to the primary task of the organization and how it is possible for these elements to become uncoupled, thereby leading to organizational dysfunction.

Following on from this, it is possible to create a further triangle of coach, coachee or client, and organization (Figure 1.2) as a way of conceptualizing the coaching system. The coach derives authority from the organization via his or her contract with it to work with the coachee. The issues the coachee brings for coaching need to be seen in the context of the organization within which he or she works and which has paid for and commissioned the coaching.

This concept helps the coach to remember to keep the coachee's organization in mind as well as the layer of meaning around the coaching system itself. In initial explorations with the coachee about the reasons for seeking coaching, the coach needs to keep in mind as many layers of meaning as possible (individual, group, organization, etc.), and this includes what it means for the coachee to be consulting this particular coach. This links to the layers of meaning described by Cronen, Pearce, and Tomm (1985).

For example, in my case, there have been expectations/fears in the coachee when I was working in an organization famous for psychotherapy services. One client, who had been encouraged to seek coaching by their organization, felt that she was seen there

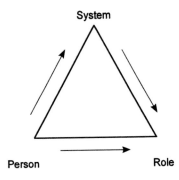

Figure 1.1. The triangle of person, role, and system (Miller & Rice, 1967a).

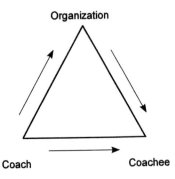

Figure 1.2. The triangle of coach, coachee, and organization (Huffington, 2006).

as "mad" and that I would be "diagnosing" her and offering her "treatment", rather than a space to think about her issues, whether individual or organizational. Another example would be the organization that offers coaching to lawyers who may become partners. The expectations associated with this particular context are well described by Noakes and Gower in their chapter about leadership development for lawyers. There is no choice about whether to have coaching, so it acquires a particular meaning connected to judgement or gate-keeping associated with the partner selection process. This can create both constraints and opportunities for the coach in exploring the potential that coaching has for helping coachees who may feel under duress.

Becoming aware of the meaning that coaching has for the coachee helps me to understand what might be missing or problematic in the organization. So how am I being used or taken up by the coachee? In the first example above, the coachee expressed very different views from others in the organization, and this tended to be construed as disruptive rather than creative. This gave clues about where the organization had got stuck in its development and had become overly rigid and bureaucratic. The coachee became anxious about the way she was seen as challenging the organization and had been labelled as difficult and sent for coaching to stop her being like this—or at least, this is how she saw it.

The "organization-in-the-mind"

The "organization-in-the-mind" is a concept developed by Pierre Turquet (1974) and subsequently by David Armstrong and colleagues at the Grubb Institute and the Tavistock Consultancy Service (Armstrong, 2005). It refers to the way the individual conceptualizes and emotionally registers the organization within him/herself. It is the organization within the individual; this may or may not be the same as the "organization-in-the-mind" of other individuals, but it will clearly bear a close relation to it. One might say that, from a psychological point of view, the organization is the sum total of the many "organizations-in-the-mind" of all who are inside or outside or in some relation to it. Thinking in this way helps one not to take for granted how the individual is thinking or feeling about his or her workplace but to remain curious about it, even if I think I know about the person's kind of work and core business. I have found it helpful in my development as a coach to be working with organizations whose core business I do not know well, simply because this means I have to ask a lot of questions about them.

Although I spent many years based in the health sector in the UK National Health Service and have my own NHS "organiza-tion-in-the-mind", I try not to assume how it feels to other NHS workers. I ask what ideas and feelings they have about it and how these contrast to when they joined; also, what made them work in the NHS in the first place? This is a way of enquiring into their primary task in being there, perhaps in contrast to the organi-zation's primary task and how they see this (Lawrence, Bain, & Gould, 1996).

For example, a client of mine is a successful CEO of a famous marketing consultancy. However, the most important aspect of his workplace to him is that it is like a family where he feels he belongs: this is his "organization-in-the-mind". He needs it to feel like this for personal reasons connected to his background, but it is clear that others feel like this too. This seems to create a sense that it is sometimes difficult to make radical changes to the busi-ness that might require a different structure or for people to leave because the bonds and allegiances to the business are more than just professional ones. The ties are more like family ties, and thus a different, more rationally based view is harder to express. One might hypothesize that it has been important or even inevitable in a creative business where a lot of money can be made that emo-tion needs to run high to succeed creatively and win the work; purely professional relationships between people would not be enough because they might be too rationally based to generate the emotional connectedness needed for creative endeavour. Of course, the downside of this is that more emotionally based work relationships blur personal/professional boundaries and personal conflict, and emotional outbursts of a potentially disruptive nature are rife in this industry, which lives at a higher emotional temperature than others. It can make sensible business decisions hard to reach except in a crisis.

This illustrates the point that the "organization-in-the-mind" can often derive from primary emotional processes associated with the work the organization does (Menzies, 1959). This refers to the emotions generated by the core business of the organization. For example, for nurses, there may be emotions of fear, disgust, sympathy, and even guilt associated with dealing with the ill and with death and dying. In investment banking, there are emotions of excitement, greed, and risk associated with making big deals involving a lot of money. It is important within the approach that I use to try to understand the "organization-in-the-mind" of the individual coachee, especially where this might conflict with what the individual or organization need to do to survive and grow.

The problem as attempted solution

Clients bring to coaching issues that they experience as problems or blockers or perhaps opportunities that they want to make the most of. Within a systemic approach, it is important to be able to see these issues as keys to unlock understanding of the organization. I like to see the individual in front of me as a representative from the organization coming to tell me what the organization has got stuck with. The individual is thus carrying something on behalf of the system. He or she is perhaps bringing "symptoms" that represent a problem or issue that is emblematic of the system's developmental issues of the time. The case example presented later in this chapter can be seen in this way.

A smaller example would be the Finance Director (FD) of a pharmaceutical company who has been told he needs to change his management style. The company is growing globally, and his centralist style is no longer appropriate for a company that will be dispersed all over the world, with local finance offices that need to be able to make their own decisions to suit local circumstances. The FD has been referred for coaching to help him change his individual style, but his increasingly controlling behaviour has been his attempted solution to the problem of how to keep control of a system that is becoming fragmented. It is a challenge to the whole company, not just the FD, although he may feel it first because of being in charge of a highly sensitive function in the business. The company needs to find a way to lead and manage in the new circumstances that does not impose more control from the centre but creates a system of governance that allows autonomy as well as regulation and monitoring.

Increasing feedback in the system

One of the things I have noticed about clients who come for coaching is that their organizations often seem to lack self-knowledge and also lack difference and diversity. They feel very stuck, and the individual's request for coaching appears to indicate a wish to bring about change in his or her own and the organization's stuckness. So anything coaches or coachees can do to increase information and feedback can be helpful. Clients can become inspired by the coach's curiosity to become curious as well and take on some homework to explore the organization, questioning his or her assumptions about how things are—for example that change is not possible. This can open up new routes to change, such as, for example, finding out why the organization has no performance management system, or what their boss thinks about their chances of promotion, or what others in the team think about their ideas about future strategy for the business.

Another way of doing this is for the coach to conduct 360-degree feedback interviews with respondents chosen by the client, usually a mix of boss, peers, and direct reports. This approach is very different from 360-degree feedback questionnaires administered annually by some organizations as part of a formal performance or appraisal process. It differs from this in that it is confidential, individually tailored, and conducted by someone external to the organization and aims to challenge and probe the views others hold of that individual and why they hold them. It is intended to help the coachee to develop an observer position both of him/ herself and the organization. Some of the questions, while jointly devised by the coach and coachee, are specifically designed to explore the organization-in-the-mind of respondents: for example, "What gets in the way of you benefiting from x's strengths [where 'x' is the coachee], in terms of either the individual him/herself or his or her role or organizational issues?" I have often found that not only does this release more feedback and information for the individual concerned, it also raises the curiosity of respondents in a useful way both about that individual and the organization. At the least, it creates a new alertness or awareness of that individual being interested in his or her development and in change, which might not have been seen before. I have often encouraged the individual coachee to go back to respondents, who will be a mix of direct reports, peers, and senior people. The discussion would not necessarily relate specifically to their feedback, which is confidential, but in general terms to what they will be doing differently as a result of all the feedback received. In several instances, this has changed a limited connection to a much better relationship.

Other ways the coach can personally increase feedback in the system are by observing the coachee at work—for example, being part of a management team development workshop in the role of observer of the client who is the CEO and giving him live feedback about his behaviour. Clearly this has to be very carefully contracted with all participants, but my experience of doing this is that it can create a context in which all participants become aware of and interested in examining their behaviour, not just the CEO. The experience of being observed helps everyone present to become more aware of how they are being seen and how they are seeing their own behaviour both as individuals and organizationally. At the end of a recent management team development workshop where I was observing the CEO, there was a discussion with all present about how the organization appeared to outsiders, with people offering their hypotheses about what they thought I was seeing as well as questions to me about this. Thus, we were sharing our different perspectives on the "organization-in-the-mind", and this led to a further discussion about what might need to change in the organization in the future.

The reflecting team

It is occasionally possible for coaches working with a number of leaders in an organization to come together as a reflecting team (Andersen, 1987) to share themes, although not individual content, with other coaches. Sometimes the organization sponsoring the coaching will be interested in receiving feedback from individual coaches to assist them in understanding the development needs of their executives. I have come across several clients like this. For example, when I was coaching a number of clients in an investment bank, I asked to set up a quarterly reflective meeting with the organizational sponsor, the Head of Learning and Development, to feed back on themes coming out of the coaching work, not confidential material relating to individual clients. This had been set up with the individual clients beforehand in that, in my initial meetings with them, I had mentioned that I would be seeking the possibility of reporting back on organizational themes to the sponsor. The clients thus engaged with me in the context of a feedback loop to the organization. Far from being a threat to confidentiality, all the clients welcomed discussing with me the kind of themes I should report back on when we met just before quarterly meetings with the sponsor; thus, it added a systemic dimension to the coaching rather than detracting from it.

For example, at one point, there was a theme of women in leadership roles finding it very difficult to assert themselves with male colleagues. When this was discussed in a reflective meeting with the organizational sponsor, a training event for women in leadership roles was developed. This may not have been the right "solution" to the "problem", but it did create a sense of a feedback loop and organizational impact from coaching, and also the possibility of creating a reflecting team of coach(es) and organizational sponsor(s) working together on the organizational meaning/impact/change possibilities arising from coaching themes.

A more developed example of the reflecting team is where a team of coaches working with a team of clients can meet with the organizational sponsor(s) and discuss themes and issues across the organization and team. This is the basis of the second case example I describe below.

Systemic questioning

I have found that a key aspect of working as an "organization coach" (De Haan & Burger, 2005) with an individual leader is to help the client see that leadership involves being able to keep the whole system in mind. This marks a critical step from being a manager of individuals or processes or a specific function or silo into being a leader who can keep the whole in mind. In practice, leaders are also managers, and managers are also leaders, so that they need to be able to switch perspectives from whole to part and back again with great flexibility. Coaching can help clients to do this by teaching them systemic thinking and practice. One of the ways to do this is by asking systemic questions. These questions, which come from systemic family therapy (Tomm, 1987, 1988), can easily be applied to work with clients in organizations in the form of "interventive interviewing". They link one-to-one work with the whole system or organization in which the client works, so as to help them develop their own systemic thinking and capacity to influence the organization in their leadership role (Hieker & Huffington, 2006). Tomm (1988) identifies certain types of systemic questioning: *lineal* questions, *circular* questions, *strategic* questions, and *reflexive* questions.

» *Lineal* questions are used to orient the coach to the coachee's situation and help him or her to investigate it. Lineal questions are factual and based on who did what/when/how/why—for example, "How old are you?" "What is your role in the organization?"

» *Circular* questions are those that try to find the patterns that connect people, tasks, beliefs, context, and so forth—for example, on hearing that the client is worried about his relationship with his boss, "Who else is worried?" "Who do you think worries the most?"

» *Strategic* questions are those that tend to open up new avenues of thinking—for example, "What has stopped you from discussing your concerns with your boss?"

» *Reflexive* questions introduce a hypothetical future scenario and encourage the coachee to take an observer perspective on his or her situation, which tends to mobilize his or her own problem-solving resources—for example, "If you were to share with a colleague how you experience the conflict with your boss, what do you think he would do?"

I would tend to use all these types of question at different points in my coaching.

For example, Kate was a consultant in a global professional services company. She was very successful with clients, but her colleagues found her brusque and uncaring. She wanted promotion, and this depended on colleagues having a good opinion of her. At our first meeting, we began with *lineal* questions about the organization where Kate worked and how she used her time. It became apparent to her that she knew little about her own organization apart from her immediate area, and she resolved to find out more. I used *circular* questions linked to her behaviour, such as, "What do you think your colleagues think about your performance with clients?" and *reflexive* questions like, "How do you think junior colleagues would react if you offered to mentor them on how to win new projects?" This resulted in Kate deciding that 360-degree feedback interviews would be useful in helping her to understand exactly what colleagues thought about her. Other questions that tuned Kate in to her impact on others were future-oriented *reflexive* questions, such as, "Where do you expect to be in five years' time?" and "How would you like to be described as a partner in the firm?" and observer-perspective *reflexive* questions like, "When you are brusque with your secretary, how do you think others feel about you?"

Kate was able to spend a few months gathering data about her organization and her colleagues and meeting them to discuss feedback about her, with the result that they formed a good impression of her interest in them and willingness to change. She was able to work to change her behaviour at work and became a partner later that year.

The case study below involved using systemic questioning to help the coachee become more aware of the whole organization.

Case example 1:
Getting the system in the room

My coaching client was Sarah, a Vice President in an investment bank. She was part of a group of vice presidents new to senior management roles who were offered six sessions of senior executive coaching as part of a management development programme. One of her development issues was her problem in making presentations to senior colleagues, as she had had feedback that she came across as unclear and unconfident. The bank would usually respond to a problem like this by suggesting Sarah went on a course to improve her presentation skills, but as Sarah believed she presented well in other situations, she thought there was more to it, so she brought it to me in our first coaching session.

I began my work with Sarah by explaining that we would explore her issue from many different perspectives and that I would need to get to know her as a person, in role, in her working group and also about her view of the organization and its challenges. This shows how I would build understanding of the layers of meaning involved in the client issue (Cronen, Pearce, & Tomm, 1985). So after some orienting questioning (lineal questions about Sarah and her role and the organization), it was possible to explore the issue, staying quite close to it initially and gradually extending the frame of reference by following the client feedback (Campbell, Draper, & Huffington, 1991). Some useful questions were:

» "What is different about presenting to senior colleagues than it is in other situations?"
» "What are you trying to achieve when you are presenting in this situation?"

Then I widened the frame of reference to:

» "Do you think colleagues have similar problems?"
» "What kind of business challenges are the bank facing right now?"

I did not ask Sarah about herself personally at this stage, for several reasons. First, it was not what she was interested in doing, as she was keen to think about her role and the organization and the task she felt she had of tackling her immediate issue. Second, I would not usually start exploring a work issue with a client by questioning about the individual as a person. I would want to keep the field of inquiry as wide open as possible at this stage, as this helps orient both the coach and the coachee to the organizational meanings of the issues brought to coaching.

We discovered that presenting to senior colleagues was anxiety-provoking for several reasons:

» it was they who would decide on Sarah's upcoming promotion

» the most difficult situation was in business unit meetings, where senior traders were not eager to hear presentations from Sarah as she was leading the operations side of the unit and, in particular, a new initiative to be more aware of risk management

» the bank was in a downturn following a lack of confidence in the investment banking world due to the collapse of Barings Bank (this was some years ago); hence Sarah's apparently personal issue represented an organizational failure of confidence

» her presentations were intended to signal a change of behaviour to traders, which they were resisting.

The anxiety they felt about scrutiny of their behaviour appeared to be experienced by Sarah, who became nervous and presented poorly as a result.

Sarah went away from the first meeting with some homework based on the curiosity she now felt about the organization rather than just herself: to check if others at her level and in her function were also experiencing similar difficulties in meetings with traders.

Next time we met, I asked Sarah how her research had gone. She had discovered that other colleagues were in fact experiencing exactly the same kind of problem. They welcomed the chance to share thinking about why this was the case. They wondered if the traders knew about the initiative to be more assertive with risk management and the role they had been given in leading this. They decided to discuss this with the Head of Operations. Meanwhile Sarah and I explored the relationship between traders and operations in the past and since the initiatives about risk management had been introduced, so that we both could better understand the resistance to change that she had encountered. Some useful questions were:

» "What is the hierarchy now in the relations between traders, operations, and other functions in the bank?"

» "How do traders see the area of risk management?"

» "If traders were to think more about the risks of the deals they make, how would this affect profits in the bank?"

She replied that, while the traditional hierarchy in the bank was traders first, then other functions (e.g., IT), and lastly operations, the new risk-management initiative was being led by operations, thus reversing the hierarchy. She thought traders did not like risk management because it would inhibit the daring they needed to do their jobs well; if they were to stop and think too much, they might get nervous, and this might affect the potential for both big risks and big wins. Risk-taking was, in fact, what gave them job satisfaction.

Next time we met, Sarah reported that the Head of Operations had taken seriously the meeting with Vice Presidents in the function. It seemed that the traders may have chosen not to know about the change in policy or that it had not been properly communicated or worked through in business units about what this might mean and how they needed to work. He undertook to meet with the Head of Trading to discuss it further.

Sarah and I worked on how she needed to prepare differently for meetings with traders now she better understood the impact of her presentations on them. It was a new idea for her that she might be making *them* anxious rather than the other way around. She decided to have more limited aims for the presentations and would present less information overall. She would prepare a few key points on cards, rather than using a large number of slides.

She anticipated some of the possible objections and prepared her responses to these. Some useful questions here were:

» "How do you think you can present so as to make the traders less anxious while still getting the risk message across?"

» "How could you initiate collaborative discussions on how to implement the new policy together?"

At the fourth meeting, we discussed progress. There had been some further organization-wide attempts to communicate the new risk policy better. She had been able to help promote some collaborative discussions about risk in the business unit as well as making some presentations, which went down well.

Sarah mentioned her remaining nervousness with senior people in the bank. Having explored the systemic background to this issue, Sarah wanted to talk to me about its personal resonance. In my experience, there is usually a personal resonance or valency in the individual to pick up on organizational tensions and register them in a personal way, the mistake being to see the issues as only personal. We therefore used part of this session to explore the significance of Sarah's issue in terms of her relationship with authority figures. She had a strict father who often used to frighten her with his violence. She tracked some of her fear in relation to senior colleagues back to her relationship with her father. This led into a discussion about men and women in the bank and the fact that there was a gender as well as functional split between traders and operations staff, traders all being male and operations staff being both male and female. The bank tended to cover up gender issues in political correctness for fear of sex-discrimination cases going to court, as had happened recently. Sarah felt these factors emphasized the traditional supremacy of traders in the bank hierarchy and was a further systemic as well as personal factor in the situation we were exploring. Some useful questions here were:

» "What other situations in your life have made you feel the way you do in presentations to senior traders?"

» "What did you do in the past that helped or did not help you that might be useful now?"

» "How does the bank address gender issues at work?"

At the fifth meeting, Sarah told me she and her colleagues were now meeting regularly to support one another with the implementation of risk-management strategies across the bank. They aimed to try to meet regularly with the Head of Operations as a kind of advisory/consultation group to help him in his large change project. She was about to enter preparation for promotion, and the assessment of her by traders in the business unit was critical. Sarah felt her performance at the meetings was now much better, but we used part of the session to plan how she would write her business case and approach the assessment meetings with senior managers, including traders.

At our last meeting, Sarah told me she had been successful in gaining the promotion she wanted. She felt she had a very different, broader view of the issue she had initially brought to coaching and, as a result of the research she had undertaken and the action that followed on from this, had acquired a support/reference group in the other vice presidents in the operations function she did not have before. She had also gained a more influential relationship with the Head of Operations because of helping to promote a wider discussion about the change issues in the bank and the difficulties of implementing new policies.

Assessment

The work done with Sarah shows that it is possible, with the right client, to provoke the person's curiosity about the organization sufficiently for him or her to, first, become more systemically aware and, second, become more active in the system to change things based on new information and feedback. It certainly improved the situation for this individual client, but was it anything more than "tinkering around the edges" of the organization? If the coach is working as an "organization coach" in this way, it could be seen as covert and not fully legitimized by the organization, rather like a kind of internal consultant (Huffington & Brunning, 1994). The impact on the organization is limited by the portal or gateway through which one has to work—in this case, a single individual and someone relatively junior in the organization.

Case example 2:
Impacting the organization

In the second case, it was possible as a coach to have some impact at the leadership level of the organization, as it involved coaching of members of the top management team of a global IT company. This work had the potential to build the "critical mass" of debate and challenge that the CEO needed to bring about larger-scale change in the organization's leadership and overall business direction.

The company had begun as a start-up four years before and had doubled its profits in that time and spread its operations across the world. It was facing opportunities for further growth but also huge challenges about how to develop the organizational structure and leadership and management capability to run the larger, more complex organization. The top management team of ten directors in particular still had the casual style of the start-up they were four years ago and operated as a group of representatives of silos or divisions and functions within the organization, with the CEO very much in charge. As a growing company, this way of operating was no longer fit for purpose. The CEO was planning to leave, so he needed to develop successors; team members themselves needed to develop the next level down as they stretched themselves to cover larger and larger areas of responsibility as the company grew; and the team as a whole needed to act corporately and collaboratively to develop a holistic vision and shared strategy for the future of the company.

The company had no history of leadership and management development, and only a few of them, who had come from other companies, had experienced coaching. An external consultant had advised that the top team needed development in its leadership of the company and so did the individuals within it. This was not taken forward. At this stage, the CEO and top team did not seem to see a business case for it—they did not make a connection between personal/team development and company profitability. It appeared a distraction from important operational issues and was therefore not prioritized.

Nevertheless, the HR Director, a member of the top team, hired a group of coaches to work with members of the top team, including herself. I was asked to coach the HR Director. Then began the difficult task of encouraging engagement in the process by other members of the top team. The CEO did not take the lead, so it was difficult to get the attention of the others. Eventually, after six months, one or two members of the team, notably those who had experienced coaching before, engaged with their coaches. They were perhaps attracted by the design of the programme. It was to begin with 360-degree feedback interviews followed by six coaching sessions. The feedback interviews were to be conducted by the coach on behalf of the coachee and would include peers, direct reports, and the CEO.

Regular meetings of the coaches with the HR Director were also part of the package. The purpose of these meetings was to share themes, not specific content, coming out of the individual coaching as well as to update coaches on information about the organization. Initially these meetings were marked by frustration: how would this initiative ever take off if the CEO was not involved or was apparently not interested? Those who were receiving coaching seemed to feel frustrated, too—that the CEO was a "control freak" and that top-team meetings were dysfunctional because they were so dominated by him that no one else got a look-in. They tended to be working at far too operational a level and not developing the next level down. They felt in need of more time, attention, and coaching from the CEO but rarely met him. He was also far too involved in detail and not strategic enough. There was a need for a debate in the senior team about leadership development, but it did not happen. We also learned that a key project had begun to track gaps in recruitment, identify star performers, and define potential successors to the CEO.

Examining the dynamic in the team of coaches was also instructive. We were a competitive group with conflicting views on what was going on in the organization and who was to "blame". Some of the coaches had been hired by top-team members themselves rather than by the HR Director; I was the only coach who was a member of an organization, and I was the only one (unknown to the others) being paid to attend the coaches' meetings. The interaction between us seemed to mirror the unacknowledged competition in the top team as well as its diversity and hidden allegiances, particularly with the CEO, who tended to manage them as individuals rather than as a group; thus the top team was more like a collection of individuals who had one-to-one relationships with the CEO rather than being a collaborative team.

As time went on, the critical intervention appeared to be the 360-degree feedback interviews and the analysis of the themes from these interviews in the coaches' meetings. As most coachees included in their respondents other members of the top team including the CEO and sometimes external stakeholders including Board members, everyone started to get involved in the process of developing more feedback in the system. After a few months, management development as a key organizational priority appeared on the Board agenda, so the CEO now had to take notice. It seemed that the Board took a different position in relation to management development, which allowed the CEO to change his. Some of the questions that were asked in the feedback interviews oriented respondents to organizational issues such as:

» "How is x [coachee] dealing with the challenges and opportunities facing the organization right now?"
» "How is x developing the next level down?"
» "How can x develop more influence in the organization?"

Themes in coaches' meetings about a year into the project included the need to be patient and let the flow of feedback do its work. More people in the top team were signing up for coaching or feedback, and there was much in the feedback about continuing frustration with the functioning of the top team and the style of leadership adopted by CEO, and the need to work more collaboratively and get out of the detail. Pandora's box could not be closed and the messages could not be put back in. The "seeping model"—as members of the coaches' meeting called it—now seemed to be slowly working.

The next significant event was that the CEO asked to meet me to talk about some of the feedback coming out of the 360-degree feedback interviews which had reached him. In particular, he was concerned about complaints that top-team members were too controlling, even bullying, in their management style. He thought this might be a factor behind poor recruitment and retention of senior people in the organization because people were unhappy with the organizational culture. This information was part of the results of the recent project and touched upon his key concerns about his own succession and the survival of the company in the future. He wanted help from me about how to discuss this feedback in his meetings with his direct reports in upcoming appraisal meetings. At this meeting, I asked him if he thought his team members were behaving like this because this is what they thought he wanted. He was very shocked and started asking me how he thought they were seeing him. He seemed concerned at the idea that he might be seen as a bully or too controlling. This provided an opportunity to suggest he might like to have feedback interviews conducted about him. Shortly after this meeting, I was asked by him to undertake 360-degree feedback interviews and coaching for him personally. This began with collecting feedback from top-team members and others in the organization, including Board members, and then meeting the CEO to develop a personal action plan based on the developmental areas outlined by respondents to the process. So the CEO at last got personally involved in the developmental work, which would perhaps enable a wider discussion of changes needed in leadership and direction in the company as a whole.

Assessment

This work demonstrates how it is possible to build, in the system, a critical mass that can generate feedback that can bring about change. But in this case it was not fast, as the whole process to date has taken 18 months! The critical mass involved in the coaches' meetings was working to make sense of the systemic forces at work. This involved the impact of the developmental work with members of the top team and their increasing ability to voice their frustration in the senior team. However, this came together with concerns about recruitment and retention in the company reflecting dissatisfaction at lower levels and the concerns of the Board about the organization's readiness for the future. So the critical mass involved a desire for change at all levels in the company, but the increased feedback allowed this desire to be voiced and shared; thus the coaching work provided a catalyst for change. The information about change in different parts of the system that was shared in the coaches' meetings and the hypotheses and systemic formulations we developed together informed each of us in our work with individual coachees, thus creating feedback loops that incorporated more and more systemic information over time. This eventually escalated into piquing the curiosity of the CEO, but I would say that the "tipping point" (Gladwell, 2000) was the involvement of Board members. I would like to think that some of the questions that I asked enabled them to link profitability to management development in such a way that it became an urgent issue. For example, "Can you describe x's capability and skills in developing the next level down so as to release him for more strategic work?" or "What will happen if the organization is unable to develop credible successors for the CEO when he leaves?" When management development got on the Board agenda, it rose up the list of priorities for the CEO and suddenly made its own business case, rather than being a "nice to have but not to do" that could be ignored.

The coaches' meetings would not have taken place at all without the influence of an imaginative HR Director who created a collaborative system for thinking about management and leadership in the organization. This group mirrored the working group that the top team needs to become. In that sense, it is a kind of simulation—not that it was planned in this way, but its laboratory style of working helped the process of engaging the top team in development in the same way that the top team itself needs to work to engage the organization in its development.

One could argue that the coaches got too interested in a particular outcome—that is, engaging the team and its members in coaching—rather than being interested in why they were so interested in this outcome and what this represented about the organization. I think I got caught up in this too, as if I could only be valuable if I was coaching more members of the team or if I won the "prize" clients, including the CEO. Thinking about it now, I think it has something to do with the company goal of innovation in IT. This is where the excitement and motivation come from and how the people there are skilled and rewarded. They have difficulty in staying with and developing products once created, whether this is in terms of their worldwide operation or in terms of people in the organization. They are keen to get on with the next big idea and keeping on moving. The coaches' team, while it did get caught up in discussing moving forward all the time, was nevertheless able to think about the internal resources of the organization and how they could be developed so as to sustain the future growth of the company.

Conclusions

So does this mean that all coaches are frustrated organizational consultants trying to influence at one step removed? Taking a step back from this question, the job description of a coach working within a systemic framework is not an organizational consultant by another name. However, if one sees one's role as helping one's client to develop an awareness of him/herself as a member of an organization and new perspectives on his or her authority to act in role, then this may result in changes in the organization. It is otherwise too indirect and limited a role—unless one is working with the top leader of an organization or with large numbers of more junior people—to be able to have an influence on wider organizational change. And, indeed, clients come for coaching with an issue that they often see as very personal, and usually it is both personal and organizational. Following the client's feedback and curiosity is vital, and some clients are more interested than others in exploring links between their issues and the organization, although this can change over time. Sarah happened to be very interested in the organizational meaning of her "problem" and keen to approach it in this way from the start. Other clients might be different. In the second example, the coaching work took place within a framework designed by the organizational sponsor to have a wider impact.

A second related question to the above is whether it is more difficult these days for those leading organizations to think and act systemically. This may, paradoxically, be why they seek a one-to-one intervention in the form of coaching. Performance targets and high pressure on leaders may produce a situation where people experience organizations very individually. There is a lack of a sense of community and of being able to rely on corporate thinking, even though many organizational goals can only be reached by teamwork or collaborative behaviour across the organization (Cooper & Dartington, 2004). It seems to be the case that those entering senior leadership roles need to be able to keep the whole organization in mind and think systemically in a way they have not had to do before. If a coach can help them to do this, it is not the same as the coach being an organizational consultant; however, it may involve the coach helping the leader to take a consultative stance in relation to the organization.

In the second case example, it was as if the organization was so fused with its task that it had lost a sense of the informal or "sentient" system of developing people to be able to do tasks and thus ensure the sustainability of the organization as well as the creative ideas it seeks to exploit. The downsizing of organizations and the removal of layers of management seems to mean that those left in leadership roles have bigger and bigger jobs with more and more tasks. The parts of their roles that had to do with being aware of people and their needs just gets "lost". This function is perhaps outsourced to the external coach and is only seen as business-critical when there are not enough managers and leaders to fill posts or when the management style is not fit for purpose in a new organizational context. The role of the coach here is perhaps to be able to help clients become more aware of both the task and people side of a leadership role and to bring this awareness of emotion into the life of the organization.

CHAPTER TWO

The collapsed-chair consultation: making moments of significance work

Christine Oliver

Commentary

Christine Oliver's chapter focuses on the core interest of systemic practice in the relationship between context and meaning. It is in framing the context that we decide what a particular behaviour means. She has become interested in the effect of the moral dimension on the way we decide what something means or on what she calls "the interpretive act". The moral dimension consists of the implicit rules of what is acceptable or legitimate behaviour or action. Oliver hypothesizes that there is a key moment in communication where a choice is made about how an interpretive act will determine future contexts.

Oliver's chapter homes in on key moments in a consultation process over three meetings. She allows us to see how the thought processes of the systemic consultant are formed at a granular level and, in doing so, makes it clear that these are jointly constructed in a complex way by all those present in the system at the time. She draws our attention to her alertness as a consultant to "incongruity between felt experience and verbal language" and how important this is to signalling areas of conflict or difficulty that cannot be voiced—for example, when the long-planned consultation had two absentees at the first meeting.

The "key moment" of the chapter title involved one of the staff sitting in a chair at work that then collapsed. The staff member brought her feelings of upset about this to the consultation. The lack of reaction to her distress appeared to be impossible to acknowledge but appeared to signal "no one cares". Oliver explains how this kind of pattern is a form of "strange-loop" communication. In this case, it is what she calls a "pseudo-charmed loop" in which members of a system are continually giving each other contradictory messages, leading to stuckness as well as instability.

Oliver's special contribution to the book is to highlight and link micro- and macro-aspects of the communication process and to provide a framework for making sense of it. This is clearly explained and illustrated in the case example. The "incongruity" cue is a useful one for all consultants using a systemic approach to signal a point of tension or difficulty in the system that cannot be discussed. Another important aspect of systemic practice illustrated in this chapter is the refusal to make decisions for consultees even when, or perhaps especially when, they are stuck and distressed—for example, when the two members of the team were absent for the first consultation meeting. Instead, Oliver exercised leadership of the consultation by offering a meta-communication about what seemed to be happening, and this allowed the team to take leadership for itself. It has to be said that a team has to be ready for this kind of approach—as this team did indeed seem to be, in acknowledging their confusion about a way forward from the start—as it requires patience and care. It is interesting to note the moral dimension in the work of the team as a Christian-based organization and the interest in morality in the consultant they chose to help them find the meaning in their team dysfunction. [Eds.]

This narrative of a consultation describes aspects of the meaning-making and action of a consultant working with a small voluntary organization where abilities to make decisions in the day-to-day living of the work have broken down. An account is created of key moments in the consultation. This is achieved by examining the links between consultant responses, the contexts that produce them, the consequent decisions to act, and their effects. These connections are considered with reference to a framework for moral reflexivity in systemic consultation practice informed by a social constructionist orientation (Campbell, 2000; Cronen & Pearce, 1985; Oliver, 1996, 2005).

Locating moral reflexivity in systemic practice

Historically, a core interest for systemic practice has been in the relationship between context and meaning (Bateson, 1972). It is a framing or labelling of the context that helps us to make sense of a situation or communication and to make choices about the next action to take. For instance, in a relationship, when one person cries, the other may need to determine whether the communication should be taken as a request for understanding, or a request for action of some kind. Bateson proposed that the interpretation of the meaning (e.g., of crying) will be contingent on the contexts of time, place, and relationship. He also distinguished between the content of an utterance and how the utterance is performed—the nonverbal dimension of the communication. In his double-bind theory he proposed that where the content and process of a communication are incongruous, disturbing consequences can be created: the contradictory message becomes internalized and later is expressed in a psychiatric condition. For instance, if the person crying is a child and the mother speaks words of comfort but communicates coldness through the way she holds the child, these contradictory messages could feel disturbing, especially if repeated over time and there are no "rules" in the system that legitimize meta-communication.

While Bateson's writings could be said to imply individual moral responsibility for communication, his double-bind narrative focuses more on the way the system positions the individual. Cronen and Pearce, working to connect social constructionist and systemic theory and practice (1985), develop Bateson's conceptualization of context and meaning in their work on coordinated management of meaning (CMM) theory. First, they enrich the use of the notion of context by proposing that contexts are multiple, multilayered, and in circular relationship. They extend the original Batesonian model of content and process by proposing that the contexts of societal discourse, family/organizational culture (implicit in Bateson's reference to tertiary injunctions about meta-communication), relationship, and identity definition will also be influential in shaping the meaning of communication. In these terms, the meaning of an incident of crying within a communication episode will be contingent on societal discourses such as those about gender, parenting, and emotion and on discourses about family culture, relationships, and identity. Furthermore, the details of the episode of communication will give clues for making meaning and action. The individual will be affected by what has gone before in the communication and will have expectations about what will follow.

Second, Cronen and Pearce develop a vocabulary for considering the moral dimension of the ways we make meaning and take responsibility for action. They point out that the contexts that shape meaning and action carry with them "rules" for what counts as legitimate, obligatory, entitled, and forbidden. For instance, I may feel I am entitled to cry in front of my partner but may feel less entitled to cry in front of my daughter; these ways of constructing my social reality will have been influenced by the contexts invoked above (and maybe others), and the ways that I take up my responsibility for action will implicate identity, relationship, and culture for self and other(s). Cronen and Pearce advocate that it is helpful in understanding communication to consider what context is having the strongest influence in any given situation and how the contexts of influence relate to each other, to the episode, and to the interaction in the episode.

In a recent book (Oliver, 2005), I develop this model and describe the *interpretive act* as a metaphorical place or space for exercising moral reflexivity. Through introducing the notion of the interpretive act, I invite reflexive consideration of one's emotional response to a communication, the meaning made of the communication one is responding to—particularly in terms of what kind of rules are invoked about what a received communication should or might mean and how one should or might respond to that meaning. In responding, we position the other with opportunities and constraints to act. For instance, if I contextualize an act of crying with the statement, "I don't need you to solve the problem but just to understand how I am feeling", it is likely that the audience to my crying will be clearer about my intentions and hopes for support. The interpretive act is shaped by a multiplicity of contexts and, in turn, shapes and reshapes further contexts for influencing emotion, meaning and action, identity, relationship, and culture.

This chapter links hypotheses about contexts of influence to the interpretive acts of the consultant in key moments of the consultation. A key moment is defined as one where the choice point in the interpretive act is felt to be crucial in determining future contexts, either by reinforcing an unwanted pattern or by providing opportunities for shaping a desired new pattern for the system. Such moments are decided through the ongoing process of observation and hypothesizing about the links between contexts, patterns, and interpretive acts. They may often be identified by an incongruity in verbal and nonverbal communication where the message verbally contradicts the message about the message nonverbally (Bateson, 1972).

Developing the meaning of "making moments of significance work"

The word *making* is used deliberately here to foreground how, within this orientation, communication is a process of participating in and building social realities (Campbell, 2000; Gergen, 1994; Pearce, 1994). The individual is treated as neither omnipotent nor impotent in shaping the opportunities and constraints of life. This approach focuses on how those opportunities and constraints are constructed or made, examining the specific contributions of a complexity of contexts and the implications of their being made in that way.

The complexity of reality is underlined. This is not an approach that thinks or acts in terms of simple cause and effect, but one that sees realities as being *made between us* through conversations in the present, inextricably linked to conversations of the past and future. In these terms, meaning is created through a complex interplay of contexts that create rules or grammars for how to interpret the episodes of communication that we are participating in, and grammars for how to act in relation to that meaning (Cronen & Lang, 1994; Wittgenstein, 1969, 1980).

The individual is seen as having powers to shape, with others, how these rules are made and, as such, is seen as having decision-making capacity of a moral nature (Cronen & Pearce, 1985; Oliver, 1992, 2005; Rorty, 1980). This is not to say that we all have equal abilities to make flexible and free choices. Rather, we must take seriously that the way we talk and listen has consequences for self and others—for our experience and for our abilities to exercise choices about how we talk about our experience. Communication in this sense is made a moral matter, implying reflexive responsibility.

Van der Haar and Hosking (2004) distinguish constructivist from constructionist approaches to reflexivity. In the former, reflexivity is an intra-cognitive activity of an individual inquirer who separates him/herself from his or her own discourse, examining his or her own assumptions, similar to what Cooperrider and Whitney (2001) refer to as the "metacognitive capacity of differential self-monitoring". In contrast, a constructionist approach to reflexivity is socio-relational and focuses attention on processes of relating, with the inquirer seen as a participant in the discourse that she or he is co-constructing (Oliver, 2005).

Reflexive positioning of self and other in the conversation lends itself to a commitment to attempting to make sense of muddles, difficult patterns, confusions, and "trouble" in communicating. The process of exploration is emphasized as much as the conclusion or outcome of exploration because knowledge is treated as never finished, always partial, only ever what can be said given the opportunities for *making sense* at that moment. For instance, decision-making about action is always a partial punctuation in the emergent narrative.

The consultant working in this tradition aspires to reflexive sensitivity about the purposes, choices, decisions, and effects of his or her communication and is interested to help others to develop the same sensibility. It is in this sense that *making moments of significance work* is being used. *Moments of significance* are identified as opportunities for constructive change created out of vital connections and disconnections between lived experience and the discourses generated by lived experience, in the process of engagement in the consultation. It is suggested that for these moments to *work*, they require morally reflexive abilities:

» in noticing and questioning actions and re-actions of participants in the conversation, including oneself

» giving meaning to what is noticed with reference to contexts of influence (such as culture, relationship, and identity narratives) and their rules for taking up moral responsibility

» noticing links and contradictions among a complexity of contexts for self and others

» coordinating feeling, meaning, and action for self and with others

» justifying one's actions with reference to the complex set of accountabilities to those involved.

Having located a frame of moral reflexivity, the question arises: how do you develop the abilities both to notice what to select out for attention and to take the forms of action that could be said to show moral reflexivity? This account of a consultation offers an example of how morally reflexive experience and reflection connect.

THE COLLAPSED-CHAIR CONSULTATION

Initial contextual information

A Christian organization in the voluntary sector, working with families in need of different forms of support, contacted me, as consultant, to help them progress their staff team functioning. The team had been able to agree that they needed a consultation but could not agree what the consultation would be for in specific terms. The initial request to the consultant, therefore, was to provide a consultation about a consultation. I was to help them reach a position where they could say what a consultation would be for. I was told in a letter from a male social worker in the team that:

» they defined their organizational structure as a "collective", with no one in an official leadership position—all were "equal"
» there was a communication problem and an inability to get to the root of it
» people would speak into the room and no one would answer
» decision-making was becoming increasingly difficult
» there was a sense of a "weight of history"
» success would count as their being able to talk about things they hadn't been able to talk about before.

It was agreed that I would work for three sessions with the team of twelve. The following does not pretend to be a comprehensive account of the work, but, rather, an examination of how sense was made of key aspects of my participation in the process and how those ways of making sense were made use of to go forward in the consultation.

Questions, stories, and connections

In preparation for the first session, I began to link together some of the information I had been given and to develop some questions so as to position myself usefully with the team. These were not questions that I would necessarily ask the team but questions I was posing to myself, linked to the beginnings of hypotheses I was developing about the complex system I was charged with helping.

» What are the contexts for deciding that the structure of this working group should be a collective?
» How is the "collective" lived out in practice?
» What is the culture of leadership in this group? How might

leadership be taken informally when there is no defined hierarchical relationship?

» How do the ways people communicate connect with shared meanings about leadership?

» How are silences understood? What effect do they have? What would need to happen for the conversation to flow and people to feel they can move forward?

» What kind of obligations, taboos, permissions, and entitlements are given and taken in the context of influential stories about justice, equality, and democracy?

» Are rights, responsibilities, and roles defined clearly? Is there agreement? Is agreement/disagreement explicit? What might the connections be between difficulty in making decisions and the ways professional and power relationships are defined?

» What will be made of how I position myself as leader of this process?

Key moments of significance

First key moment

Team members were invited to introduce themselves and their positions and roles within the team. Although three people located their work identity with reference to a role—for example, administrator, social worker—the majority of people said "I am just a team member". In these introductions there was an awkwardness communicated. My emotional feeling was one of muzziness, cloudiness, slipperiness—a sense of "I can't get a handle on this", a feeling of a communication being closed down. My interpretation of the communication was that an obligation to "be the same" influenced behaviour. However, a story of sameness and equality was being told in words while the pattern lived was already contradicting it. Varying abilities were being shown about confidence and apparent authority to speak. People spoke with different impacts and for very different lengths of time. The lack of coherence I observed during this episode sensitized me to calling it significant. Something of significance was being communicated, but at this stage I could not give a coherent account of its meaning except to notice that the theme of sameness and difference created discomfort.

Beginning to hypothesize about contexts and behaviours. In this episode of introductions, the "obedient" way team members did not draw distinctions among themselves, while at the same time indicating a discomfort, was suggestive of a shared belief that they should not, conveying an obligation to equality. I interpreted and hypothesized that loyalties to a shared story about sameness constructed a context of muddle in practice. I wondered how difference and value were communicated in this team if there were a strong cultural contextual rule that distinctions should not be drawn. My choice of action at this stage was to not draw attention to my observations and thoughts but to continue with setting the context for the consultation and to return to the theme of equality and diversity at a later stage.

Second key moment

After half an hour of discussion, I was informed that two team members were missing.

I observed that this was communicated with some awkwardness, combined with a kind of helplessness. I decided to treat the absence as significant in the context of it being presented as if it were not amenable to any decision-making process while at the same time a message of discomfort was being communicated nonverbally. Here was an opportunity for me to elaborate on leadership, definition of relationship, and decision-making narratives.

My *choice of action* here was to explore the logic of the contexts that could have produced the outcome of two absent team members when it had taken the team months to set the consultation up, wanting to ensure all team members could attend. I also chose to anticipate the potential consequences of different actions the team might now take. My intention was to help the team to reflect on and make problematic the contexts informing and creating the patterns they as a group were engaged in. Also, I wanted to express a clear act of leadership, to show through my own behaviour how authority can facilitate movement.

I explored who the absent team members were; how it had come about that the consultation was going ahead; and what its impact might be to have them absent or to stop the consultation at this point until we could reconvene. I invited the team to imagine the absent team members as an audience to this discussion and any communication the group made and to imagine how such communication might be understood. It emerged:

» that the two people absent were the only black members of the team

» that the task they were doing that "caused" them to be absent was necessary, but it need not have been they who did it

» that the absent members had themselves made the decision to do this task and that nobody else had questioned this decision explicitly

» that nobody had raised the issue of whether the consultation should go ahead given that two key members of the team were unable to come

» that the absent members often complained that some voices of the team were louder than others who were often not heard and that this inequality was thought to represent issues of gender and race

» that the team unanimously believed the consultation process should not go ahead with two team members absent

» that the exploration began to reframe meaning from "blaming of reluctant participants" to "a shared difficulty in engaging in a dialogue about decisions".

My next decision was to leave the group (as it had been agreed that we should not continue the consultation at that point). I left after engaging in a discussion of how to communicate the decision that had been made to the absent members, so that they might feel engaged in the future process of consultation.

Continuing to hypothesize about contexts, feelings, meanings, and actions.   It was striking that a story was being told of an inability, in the context of this team's culture, in speaking out as individuals or as a representative of the group. There was a theme here of everyone waiting to be led but no one legitimately able to lead; there was an inability to go on in the conversation (Wittgenstein, 1969, 1980). My sense was that a strong constraining context for this paralysis was an ambiguity about definition of relationship. In the context of confusion about rights, responsibilities, expectations, and roles and how these fitted together to make a team that functioned coherently, team members did not have sufficient clarity to identify who to speak to whom about what, and in which circumstances—a poverty of accountability. I hypothesized that in a context where leadership is not formally taken, it will be taken informally and will be constructed or (il)legitimized according to implicit criteria. Such processes create a story of disempowerment rather than "no power", which was the intention associated with the language of "the collective". Constraints were being created in the name of freedom.

What were the constraining contexts and meanings that created such ambiguity, however? This question needed greater elaboration.

In the following session, all team members were present and acted as if they were engaged in a process of consultation. However, it was striking that no one ever showed any curiosity about others' responses—there was no checking of meaning and no requests to elaborate. Everyone acted as if they knew what others meant, constraining the potential for difference or disagreement. I felt a sharp awareness of this dynamic, contrasting with my own sense of curiosity about the contexts for team members' utterances and the emotional constraint and discomfort alongside the utterances.

A theme of the importance of equality was emerging, but alongside that a feeling was being expressed of deficit and failure. This was illustrated by no distinctions being drawn about experience and professional training in terms of allocation of tasks. Some people were engaged in tasks where, on the one hand, they felt ill equipped to do them and, on the other, it was not clear to whom they were accountable. It was agreed that these contradictions would be explored in the next session, with a view to helping the group reach a point of decision-making about a future consultation.

Third key moment

Early on in the third session, a story was told by one of the black members of the group about an upset she had experienced that week. She had sat on a chair at work, and it had collapsed. She had gone home bruised and shaken, but no one had contacted her to see if she was alright. The account she was developing was that no one cared, that no one could be bothered to telephone, that no one was interested in protecting the working environment. She asked the group, who was responsible?—and no one answered. There was an eloquent silence. Everybody looked embarrassed and hurt. I felt a defensive, brittle feeling and interpreted that confusion at cultural, relational, and identity levels of context was inviting the story "no one cares" and the hurt associated with that.

My *choice of action* here was deliberately intended to stop this pattern—of feeling hurt, interpreting that no one cares, and blaming others. I believed that to continue with it would have reinforced stories of:

» the problems here are to do with people not caring
» that if you protest about this, communication will improve
» structural definitions of relationship are not relevant
» these problems are caused by misuse of power.

I linked this episode to the theme of decision-making and the developing acknowledgement of ambiguous accountability—team members not knowing whom they could count on. It was brought to the group's attention that a particular interpretation was being made about people's intentions (as not caring) that had the effect of no one knowing how to speak in relation to the accusation and feeling implicated in a sense of failure. I suggested that a story about personal motivations also distracted from any organizational gaps or muddles that could be usefully explored.

I asked the group a question next, the response to which was silence. Interpreting the silence as a request for help with how to go on, I decided to share a partially formed analysis of the behaviour of the team and my interpretation of how the contexts influencing team members' emotional responses, meaning-making, and patterns of behaviour might fit together. My intention to introduce some clarity into the feeling of miserable muddle felt justified in this atmosphere of helplessness.

I asked the group to consider how the ideas I was about to share might help their own sense-making. I made it clear that the connections I was offering were partial and rooted in my experience and that their own experience might emphasize and de-emphasize different aspects. I asked them to treat the ideas as work in progress, to add to, to change, to question, to disagree with.

I shared with the group the following links between contexts, feeling, meaning, and action:

» *Culture:* Loyalty to collective culture creates a story that all staff members are equal, which is interpreted as "we have no leaders". It also sows the seeds for a fear of conflict. This creates a context for:

» *Relationship:* Confusion of relational accountability. The loudest, experienced, confident voices are heard most, and the inexperienced are quieter. Gender and race become visible as dimensions of power in relationship. This sets a context for:

» *Identity:* Individuals experience communication and role-definition problems, and these are named as power issues—"I have no power". The confusion invites a story that no one cares.

These strong shared contexts and storylines keep the looped form of communication in Figure 2.1 going in a way that makes for a shared sense of disorientation, confusion, and tension. The narrative of this pattern goes like this: An imperative is felt that decisions must be made. However, this creates a fear that there will be conflict, which is interpreted as unsafe, thus silence or other forms of withdrawal are created. In the context of silence, a temporary harmony is created and perhaps a feeling of "pseudo-equality",

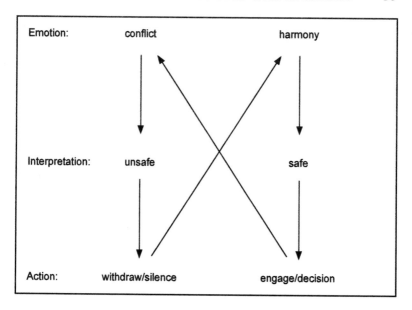

FIGURE 2.1.   A pseudo-charmed loop

which creates a feeling of safety, so moves are made towards decision. However, that sets a context for fear of conflict, so no decision is made. And so this oscillating pattern goes on.

This pattern is one form of a strange-loop pattern (Cronen,
Johnson, & Lannaman, 1982; Oliver, 2005; Oliver, Herasymowych,
& Senko, 2003). It is a figure whereby each level of context in the
loop contains its opposite and each context becomes the context
for the next, with no escape unless the powerful contexts and storylines holding it together can be noticed and transformed. Oliver
and colleagues have called such a loop, which is driven by a fear
of conflict, a pseudo-charmed loop. This oscillating loop has characteristics of the double-bind (Bateson, 1972), in that the members
of a shared system of context, feeling, meaning, and action will
be giving each other contradictory messages over time, creating a
lack of stability and a sense of moving back to the same place. As
with the double-bind, unless one can take an observer position to
it, and preferably, meta-communicate about it, system members
are destined to continue the paradoxical pattern.

As a working text, this interpretation of the problematic experience they brought to the consultation was received with great animation, creativity, and relief. People discussed their responses in pairs before sharing and building on them in the larger group. After a process of working on the pattern together, working groups addressed some key questions facing them:

» By what mechanism should they decide what to do next?
» Who should be involved in the decision?
» Do they have to agree?

The groups resolved these questions in a straightforward manner and made decisions about the forthcoming consultation, in terms of the potential topics needing further exploration, the process, and the personnel involved. They requested that the next session with the consultant should help them to prioritize their concerns and that the pseudo-charmed loop offered a starting point for thinking about different layers of team experience. They agreed that all should be at that meeting and contribute to the discussion, each person being given an opportunity to share his or her own experience of dilemmas and difficulties while others listened respectfully. The team made the request to the consultant that they be helped to prioritize the themes that emerged. If there was disagreement, that would be named and a decision made at the time about how to address it.

Discussion

The moments of significance that have been noticed and explored here have been chosen because of a sense of incongruity between felt experience and verbal language. The signal labelling the mode of communication contradicted the message received by the communication (Bateson, 1972). A framework connecting the contexts of culture, definition of relationship and identity, and the interpretive act of emotional, cognitive, and behavioural response has been used to facilitate morally reflexive action by both the consultant and the team members.

For Key Moment I, the utterance "I am just a team member" was communicated alongside the label "uncomfortable", alerting me to be interested in how relationships were defined in the context of organizational culture. I was mindful of the fragile integrity of the system at this early stage of the consultation and sensed the need for maintaining a context of clarifying the emerging definition of relationship in the consultancy process.

This positioning helped me in Key Moment II to offer authority and clarity in managing the premature ending of that session while facilitating the responsibility of the team to position themselves with greater moral reflexivity towards each other. Leadership culture and decision-making relationships were identified as significant frames for the episode. The utterance "two team members are missing" was labelled nonverbally as information for, and in, the ongoing consultancy (as if we should continue), yet it meant we were not in an appropriate context to engage in the consultancy because I would be reinforcing the message of inequality if I only engaged with some team members and not others. This contradictory message required meta-communication and disruption of the potential pattern.

Key Moment III represented a crucial opportunity to connect and integrate my observations about the patterns of engagement I had participated in, with language that could re-imagine the possibilities for the group's future by naming and re-naming those patterns with the group. The utterance "no one cares" implied that some were in a position of power and others were not and that some were to blame for the "uncaring" pattern and others were not. It was striking how consciousness of the shared systemic links in the pattern enabled movement forward. The group was able very quickly to make some decisions about the next phase of the consultation process, having previously experienced a sense of paralysis and confusion.

My choices were linked to interpreting the need for a change from personal blame to a focus on relational clarities in a confusing context of culture, relationship, and identity; the need for a shared communication frame for understanding the experience of power in the group; and the need for validation of race and gender as issues to be discussed and negotiated within the context of an understanding of the workings of relational and role entitlements and obligations.

I am taking the view here that, "how you describe a problem can make a difference and how you describe a difficulty can make a problem" (Oliver & Lang, 1994, p. 3). The view that *we make realities through the ways we communicate* sensitizes the consultant to the potential consequences of how you name a problem. In this case, it is my view that in treating the muddles and unhappiness of the team as primarily about communication and definition of relationship, and in treating the consultation as a communicative act, individuals were empowered to act as individuals and corporately and felt able to engage in the invited dialogue, but when power was positioned as the highest context for giving meaning, both the team and individuals were rendered speechless, because of the sense of threat to identity for all participants.

Conclusion

In using the device of the title "making moments of significance work", this chapter has attempted to show how the systemic practitioner creates realities (with others) through her or his abilities to communicate and make sense of how communication works. The moments of significance that have been noticed and explored have been named as such because of their potential for making use of morally reflexive processes to engage in movement forward in the work. These moments have been constructed through a form of consciousness that locates the ways voices are used (including my own) in the context of a range of moral and theoretical commitments and that translates these abilities in making sense into imaginative and accountable action.

The capacity for systemic generosity becomes co-constructed as participants come to appreciate the contextual logic for how the individual and the corporate are linked together. With this appreciation they come to rename their predicaments in ways that help them move within and through them. The significant learning for the team in this case is potentially to treat communication in a wider context than the "personal" and to develop understanding and responsibility about the ways organizational structures and definitions facilitate abilities to relate and powers to act.

This is a description of the beginning of a process of learning, and it should be said that team communication skill, structure, and strategy would need further support in changing at the level of meaning, identity, relationship, and culture to be able to say with confidence that enduring change in organizational patterns has occurred.

CHAPTER THREE

Leadership development and "close learning": reducing the transfer gap

Keith Kinsella

Commentary

The chapter by Keith Kinsella turns our attention from the thinking and methodology behind a consultation to a staff group to systemic practice in training and development. The issue facing Kinsella was how to help people transfer learning about leadership to their work contexts. The concept of "close learning" means creating and supporting learning opportunities close to or rooted in the context of performance.

Kinsella's case example is about providing shared leadership development to the separate organizations working as one organization in a local strategic partnership in the public sector in the United Kingdom. The most interesting aspect of this work is how Kinsella had to give up his original idea of offering a free-standing development programme and, in effect, to join the partnership himself in order to make a difference to the way it worked. This partly arose for practical reasons as it was impossible for the potential programme participants to release time to attend a series of separate development events; but it also demanded that Kinsella worked with the participants in the moment as they were creating their work patterns with one another, thus reducing the "transfer gap" to nil! Kinsella perhaps acted as a context marker of something different, in that he offered new ways of working that were experienced as more effective and probably unlike anything the individual organizations might have done in their own practice.

Another interesting aspect of this work is the way Kinsella conceptualized the "development sandwich" of work the partnership needed to do together. Everything they did clearly implicated other layers of their work together in a "multilevel approach to learning architecture", from intention (what they wanted to achieve in the session), context (shared assumptions and reasons for being together), process (how to work together on the issues), and content (what they needed to do—the usual focus of consultancy using other approaches). Each learning experience needed to attend to each of these layers to varying degrees so that the most was made of their time together, both developing and performing at the same time.

This approach—which resembles the approach that Simon Western describes in chapter 8 in a different setting—seems a highly cost-effective and energizing alternative to external courses or an externally imposed way of working for the new partnership organization as well as the individuals within it. It also presents a hybrid of consultation and teaching in that it was an organizational intervention to the partnership organization as well as a developmental opportunity. It is possible that this form of consultation/teaching is a new way forward for organizational development. [Eds.]

The particular issue I want to explore here is the so-called transfer problem that besets much development work: how to help people transfer what they have learned in a development or training context to their own role and work situation, in an effective and personally authentic way. One of the factors that now further complicates this issue is that managers in our slimmed-down organizations appear to have less and less time to engage in developmental activities per se. They apparently must get it on the run, so to speak, by taking part in flexible distance-learning-type programmes, or in short, sharp, offsite events squeezed within busy schedules.

What I offer here is an account of work in progress in the narrative of my learning concerned with the question: "how can I improve my practice?" (Whitehead & McNiff, 2006) in this area. As a facilitator of individual/group development in both academic and executive settings, the particular idea I have been exploring for the past few years, and wish to make the central focus of this chapter, is that of *close learning*:[1] how to create and support learning opportunities that are "close"[2] to the context of performance. Achieving this reduces the challenge of applying the learning at work and brings into focus the relational and contextual implications of personal and organizational development, as well as the cognitive and behavioural. Here I offer some reflections on my experience of early steps in developing a methodology for extending close learning ideas initially developed in Master's degree studies into the more unruly environment of facilitating development work with a local strategic partnership based in southern England.

Seeking "roots":
learning many ways of knowing

But before I look at the idea of close learning, what is my starting point with systemic thinking? Since the mid-1970s I seem to have spent a huge amount of time exploring the "why/what/how" of effective learning/development for managers in organizations. For a time during the late 1990s, I thought I was getting quite close with a particular form of action inquiry using systemic and social constructionist ideas associated with the family therapy tradition; managers seemed to get a lot of learning from intense colleague "inquisitions and gossipings", which they seemed able to embody, try out, and adapt in the light of feedback. A decade later, in trying to capture this continual search for new ideas that might provide insight into human behaviour in organizations, I came up with the metaphor "searching for roots in the future". Though this seemed a little strange at the time, I later reflected that:

> over the years one of my central yearnings has been to find (or now I'd rather say, shape with others) a more integrated, authentic, connected, and rooted me. And so perhaps this

unceasing search of mine throughout my adult career since
leaving South Africa, for new ideas over a very wide and
diverse range of topics could be seen in this light—not just
a search for better methods of consulting/coaching as I'd
thought, but more importantly, a search for roots, for a me
that would feel grounded, confident, and at home. [Kinsella,
2003, p. 8]

More recently, I have started to think about this search metaphor
as less about roots and more about rooting. This new framing
brought home to me the active responsibility I have in this process.
Rather than stumbling across sundry "roots" in my work with
others (often after the fact), I felt I was involved more in a process
of actively trying to create/establish roots as I talked with clients
or students, to do with *becoming* someone who is responsive, invi-
tational, and able to help create a culture of inquiry—that is, an
atmosphere where people are ready to challenge their own beliefs
and assumptions.

Given the many roots that have shaped this emerging epistemology, I have over the years embraced the notion of there being
many ways of knowing. As a way of trying myself to understand
interactions from many vantage points, I have tried a number of
perspectives like systemic thinking (Keeney, 1983), social constructionism (Gergen, 1999), power relations (Foucault, 1980), complexity theory (Stacey, 2003), and so on. Through using one or more
of these at any time to understand a situation, I have been able
to some extent to loosen the grip of common-sense ways of looking at things. And when I have found novel and fruitful ways of
knowing a particular interaction, I have been able to share these
perceptions with colleagues and clients to think differently themselves about something (usually without labelling whatever the
insights were for me) to some useful effect.

I now look at this loose ecology of ideas (Bateson, 1972) as a
systemic mindset that I and others can use to "fuzzy up" our first
automatic punctuations of a situation and assess just how robust
our initial perceptions might be in the glare of the multiple lights
offered by the mindset. I see this not just as set of tools but as an
"artifact" (Ilyenkov, cited in Burkitt, 1999), something that effectively extends my body-mind and allows me to engage deeper-

level tacit processes in a creative way. Here is one possible story of how I might use these perspectives to build up a multilayered appreciation of a particular situation:

» Starting position: *as objective observer*—"that's the problem/ truth/facts!"

» First move—*into double-loop learning:* "what I see ('that's the problem', etc.) is *part* of the problem" (Keeney, 1983).

» Second move—*into narrative:* "what I tell myself I see, isn't *it*—it's a *story* about *it* that gives *it* meaning" (Gabriel, 2000).

» Third move—*into social construction:* not only is it a story, it is storying constructed in language with others, where words get their meaning from use within "language games" (Gergen, 1999).

» Fourth move—*into power relations:* these constructions are legitimated/given truth value within asymmetric relations constituted by dominant narratives that embody power relations and legitimate certain views over others (Foucault, 1980).

» Fifth move—*into tacit knowledge:* these legitimated narratives are constructed largely through embodied, tacit, and metaphoric "thinking/doing" processes that to a significant extent are hidden from consciousness (Lakoff & Johnson, 1999).

» Sixth move—*into complexity:* these unconscious thinking/doing processes have the characteristics of complexity with non-linear causation and emergence (Stacey, 2003), which allow the possibility of creating possible futures in the present (or "presencing": Scharmer, 2006).

» Seventh move—*into process metaphysics:* constructing possible futures involves me/us in making "arbitrary" punctuations on the basis of "fleeting moments" within a complex background process (Wood, 2005)—for example, "that *is* the problem/truth/facts!"

So though I am back to what looks very much like my first perception, I have moved some way from the simple "that's the problem" of Step 1 to a richer and more complex appreciation of what might be influencing what's going on. And in making these perceptual moves I have established many inter-linkages between them: they are no longer isolated sequential "things" but part of a more dynamic understanding, pointing to several different lines of inquiry and encouraging me to keep open to the possibility of a range of emergent outcomes. In practice, of course, I do not use these ideas as a checklist or linear formula! They are very much at the back of my mind, as I rely on close attention to, and my tacit appreciation of, the situation to reach intuitive assessments—which I can then explore more systematically (as well as systemically!)

More recently, I have come across other ways of knowing—for example, "women's ways of knowing" (Belenky, Clinchy, Goldberger, & Tarule, 1997)—and have begun to realize that this notion of ways can also be used at a much more micro-level, in the sense of a way of knowing in a *particular* relationship. So what I am doing when I use say, social constructionist thinking *is* this, but it also is about helping the other discover/create his or her very *own* way of knowing—something I am exploring with my MA students. So this use of systemic thinking seems to offer value at both micro- (individual) and macro- (situation/context) levels of application.

Crafting partnership infrastructure: facilitating "systemic presencing"?

Over the past year, a colleague and I have been exploring the further development of the close learning idea beyond our work with mature students studying for a higher degree: we have been offering a less structured and emergent programme of development, with improving *leadership in partnership* as the focus, to groups of executives working in what is called a local strategic partnership (LSP).

The LSP is a new type of organization set up by the government to refocus the delivery of services to meet local community needs that conventional local authorities and statutory agencies like primary care trusts (PCTs) are having difficulty meeting.

These partnerships typically involve the local authorities, as well as police, PCT, education, voluntary, business, and other sectors who come together to identify, resource, and deliver more integrated "community" services, in areas such as the disadvantaged young, the vulnerable elderly, crime and disorder, and local tourism. The government has stated that it believes "the future is local", and by continuing to devolve power to these cross-sector local partnerships (ODPM, 2005), they are hoping that services to local communities will become more relevant, joined up, innovative, and cost effective. They are also hoping that these partnerships will be able to play a much stronger *place-shaping* (ODPM, 2005) role, to do with creating a much stronger and vibrant sense of local identity.

These LSPs face substantial challenges in providing appropriate leadership in partnership in their local areas. They have to: engage and weld together partners who can speak for all sectors of the community; make sense of, attenuate, and integrate multiple government policies from above and align them with local needs in appropriate local policies and plans; find funding from a confusing array of already committed and alternative new sources; and martial projects and resources to deliver these now more focused services and events in a more joined-up manner. And they need to do this in roles that are almost all of a part-time and voluntary nature, with many other demands for their time and energy.

This has confronted us with significant challenges of our own as we have looked for ways of supporting the improvement of leadership in a large and diverse group of very busy people who all wear several hats. Two incidents that happened during the lengthy orientation phase at the end of 2005 (involved in clarifying what was needed and working out how to resource this) illustrate the kind of difficulties faced:

1. By chance we were asked to facilitate an important agenda item for the executive group during one of their fortnightly meetings. This involved prioritizing and distilling well over a hundred key targets that together constituted the guts of the new Community Strategy, which they had been struggling

with for some months. Though not initially seen as part of our emerging development contract, we and they found that the approach we helped them follow had a tremendous impact on the quality and speed of their work together. It was:

- "more contexted"—for example, we used an orienting discussion to figure out what the local community was expecting from the Community Strategy;
- "more inquiring"—for example, we offered regular and timely use of questions to direct attention to the implications and likely consequences of the various options and actions being considered (e.g., how are the members of your two district councils likely to react if you do group all the detailed targets they've identified into one large theme?);
- "more fluid"—for example, we encouraged the group to abandon their usual "round the board table" process and move flexibly about the room, forming/reforming in different subgroups, as they worked on distilling the huge amount of information before them.

After only two hours of working in a more creative and flexible manner, they were able to find ways of grouping and prioritizing the hundred or so issues and reduced these to just eight strategic themes that they felt captured the challenges ahead! These themes covered such overarching aims as "Build a stronger, safer community" and "Alleviate poverty and reduce health inequalities". It was clear to all of us at the end of that short session that loosening the chains of the bureaucratic process was an important factor to consider, enabling the group to make much better use of their substantial shared tacit knowledge.

2. The second centred around the difficulty of actually finding any dates to do the development work they had recruited us to do. We were looking for start-up days with each of the groups, and time for interviewing, but found that the partners' diaries were already so crowded for months ahead that the only time that was available were *existing* dates for meetings with full agendas. So the second realization was that if we were to do any development work with these groups, it would have to be

done *while* they worked on the existing business agendas for these meetings.

These challenges pushed us to further develop our thinking down the *close learning* route, and they illustrate two important aspects associated with this approach: many people can now only do development on the run, so to speak, either *while* they are working or in short sessions during the working day, in contrast to the asynchronous nature of the e-learning approach used on our Master's programme at Exeter University; furthermore, these managers need to learn *in time* and *on the job*, and tackling key business issues in the workplace can and needs to provide a rich source of development opportunities, with learning being applied and embedded in the appropriate performance context.

So like our university work, engagement with the LSP has turned out to be very much about learning together about leadership-in-action. Since the first priority-setting session, we have now taken part in a number of successful events with the Board and Executive groups, where resolving a pressing strategic issue has provided the central focus for learning, and where participants have been able to make significant shifts in attitude and behaviour. Some quotes from a variety of those involved illustrate the kind of change that has taken place:

» *Head of Policy in Borough Council:* "The development days helped us crack 'killer issues' and to move on faster than we would have thought possible."
» *Voluntary-sector representative:* "This programme has helped us reposition ourselves in a very positive way."
» *Vice-Chair of Board:* "We have now done what we always wanted to do, which is to move from talking to action and consider and deal effectively with leadership issues. The programme has supported creative conversations."

It has become apparent that there are many "layers" involved in getting this process to work effectively. One tool we have developed to assist with this is what we now call a *development sandwich*, which, though using straightforward techniques, employs a multilevel approach to create learning architectures that support this kind of intense working/learning experience. Figure 3.1 illustrates one version, and works as follows:

1. *Intention.* At the outset, and again at the end, a commitment is reached about the learning goals and the need to spend some time reflecting and distilling what has been learned about the content, process, context, and immediate implications for their leadership roles and communications to others. Though this may seem obvious and straightforward, it is not something such groups naturally spend any time on.

    For our first development day with the Board, we helped them agree in the opening session over breakfast that after three years of being a "talking shop", the LSP had reached a critical point: it could either start to deliver something or unravel! Through involving the group in identifying and grouping what individuals wanted to get out of their work with the LSP, we were quickly able to elicit and concretize a range of important learning outcomes that people felt, if achieved on the day, would start to make a difference—for example, what would different groups in the community be noticing if the LSP started "delivering", what would "a move to action" look like inside the boardroom at meetings/this meeting, and so on.

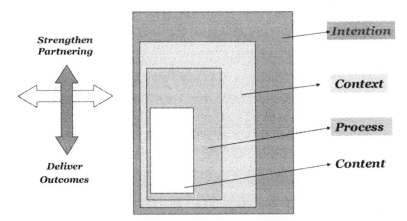

Figure 3.1.   The close learning "development sandwich": a multilevel layered approach to "developing while doing".

2. *Context.* A second layer is devoted to "contexting/relational/ visioning" work, which seeks to alter the way managers frame the issue and commit to resolving it. Often members feel they attend meetings as isolated individuals to represent their sector in some way. It takes time and effort to dig beneath the surface of usual interaction to develop the different reason(s) that bring them together, to make visible the tacit assumptions that lead to conflict or non-involvement, and to start helping members see their personal responsibility in creating the "we" within the multiple "I's" that constitute the group.

> *We discovered that most members had only a very slight acquaintance with their colleagues, formed entirely in very formal meetings. Furthermore, there had been little recent discussion about the context in which the LSP was working—issues on the quarterly agendas were dealt with almost as "context-free" matters. Though everyone was attending on a voluntary basis, no one knew why others were making this commitment. So the purpose of this session was to help colleagues situate themselves in the here-and-now: why are we here, what are the challenges we face, what do we want to do about this?" For example, in this session:*

> - *We asked each member to explore in pair interviews what they really wanted the LSP to achieve and then, on their own, to create a collage made from a selection of photos we had provided and capture this in a short story. This session provided a much clearer focus for ensuing discussions and helped deepen the level of frankness.*
> - *We offered members an initial "strategic map" covering other government, agency, and LSP groups working in the area— community stakeholders and providers, current initiatives, and so on—and got them to build their own more particular, detailed, and up-to-date version. The conversations during this process made them aware of some very real differences within the group—for example, the role of the Community Forum, a loose group of some 75 people who were expected to represent all the bodies not currently on the Board. As a result of the discussion, the group agreed this role had to be strengthened and relations with the Board improved through cross-attendance, briefings, and so on.*

3. *Process.* A third layer attends to the "methods/processes" to be used. As touched on earlier in this chapter regarding the work to prioritize targets, we employ here a range of more inquiring, participative, and creative methods that encourage and liberate managers to make better use of their experience, tacit knowledge, and ideas, both individually and as a group. We find that by constraining the usual formal meeting patterns and encouraging more risk taking and informality, people are able to share knowledge and ideas more easily, and they surprise themselves in how effectively and quickly they are able to tackle even quite complex issues.

> *Given our experience at the start of the project, we again offered the group an overall process that levelled the "influence" field and encouraged a freer, more creative, and emergent frame for a range of different conversations. We did this by, for example, replacing the normal chairing of the meeting with a number of more facilitative roles; giving everybody regular opportunities to say their piece using Post-it notes and working in smaller groups; taking regular time-outs to take the temperature and get the group to reflect actively on the process ("what seems to be emerging now?"); and through using simple voting processes ("put your three red dots on those ideas you wish to concentrate on") encouraging the will of the group to emerge more clearly. On several occasions we used systemic questions to help the group clarify the dynamics of the situation they seemed to find themselves in—for example, "how do you experience the 'contextual forces' you seem to be reacting to in this discussion?" or "what potential do you see in what you could do together in this meeting today, to strengthen the 'implicative forces' (Pearce & Cronen, 1980) and so change your sense of powerlessness by bringing desired future patterns of interaction into the room?" (Scharmer, 2006). People seemed pleasantly surprised at the consequent level of engagement and range of powerful ideas coming from previously non-committal members*

Both of these intermediate layers—context and process—are revisited from time to time during the workshop sessions, depending on how the dual-level work on content/learning is going.

4   *Content.* The central layer, the meat-in-the-sandwich, is devoted to resolving the central strategic issue, with everybody working creatively together to achieve a good outcome, using the processes agreed, the context that has been co-created, and the learning intentions to shape, energize, and support an enhanced level of effective dialogue

> *In this first meeting with the Board, we worked on the central issue of finally shaping and deciding on a set of core actions that would constitute a credible Community Strategy for the LSP, something that most of them felt was many a meeting away. However, a range of important decisions was reached, including agreeing several significant and controversial changes in the role and relationships of the three key bodies of the LSP. After years of following the mainly local-authority-staffed Executive group, the Board suddenly seemed to find its own voice and place its stamp on what was to go forward for public consumption and action. And even more surprisingly, there seemed to be general agreement that the previously low-profile Community Forum group had to be brought much more to the fore in engaging and empowering the community. The outline strategy was agreed, and five major priorities were established for funding and action in Year 1.*

Figure 3.1 illustrates the "Russian doll" or "nested" nature of the process, with each layer being designed to serve a purpose that then needs to be dynamically linked to the other layers in the light of the content that is actually emerging. For example, in this first session over breakfast, what became very clear early on was the level of frustration that many were feeling about lack of progress on achieving outcomes and about the need within the "content" layer—despite the fact that we were to talk about a ten-year strategy—to focus particularly on translating ideas into concrete actions in the short term. Furthermore, regarding our intention to work more freely in the "process" layer, it was clear we would need to focus more on the attenuation aspect rather than the amplification of ideas for action.

These four steps are principally about setting the group up to do good work on their agenda item. This *performing* process is shadowed all the way by the *developing* perspective: what are the rules and behaviours that seem to be improving/blocking progress, what are the skills the group is using/could use/needs to learn to raise their performance, and so on. These two processes—doing the work successfully and identifying development opportunities to increase capability and performance—are both "on the screen" throughout, with one or the other being foregrounded when appropriate. So on the following development day with the Executive, we used their discussion of how to position what they called "cross-cutting projects" to illustrate the power of creating a "strategic storyline" for communicating their ideas to the Board and others. A typical "cross-cutting" project involved using alcohol abuse to address in significant ways five of the eight "strategic themes" in a high-profile and concrete piece of work. This enabled them in the moment to clarify their arguments and to understand the importance of contexting their communications, while working with this tool.

In this process, we ourselves have been taking up what is very much a group coaching role. At times it has felt very much as though we have been jointly crafting with the client a group "artifact" (Burkitt, 1999), a new way of thinking about purpose and strategy and how best to embody this in an emergent future. As Keith Grint (2001) has suggested, leadership can usefully be thought of as a series of "arts" rather than a science, and this raises the question about whether learning about leadership is analogous to that of the creative artist—that is, as Lyotard (1984) puts it: one "who works without rules to create rules in the work that will have been done". This seems very much to be the essence of a "close learning methodology" (CLM) that we are evolving as we reflect *through* the work we are doing together, creating the rules as we learn from what has been done.

In addition to the framing and design challenges involved, CLM places significant demands on the group-coach resource. In the field situation, group coaches need to be able to make in-the-moment shifts across a wide variety of roles and levels, to support what the client group needs there and then, in a timely and appropriate way, as well as attend to the emergent development process. Despite the fact that clients can be negative about having two of us, it also seems clear that it pays to work in pairs, much as the early Milan School therapists did (Palazzoli, Boscolo, Cecchin,

& Prata, 1978), sharing the performing/developing demands on a fluid basis.

* * *

As a result of our experience on this assignment, we have come up with a new way of framing the process of developing leadership in partnerships. We feel it can be likened to a process of *stitching the fabric of infrastructure.* This metaphor connects many of the thoughts we have had during the past year:

» Leadership in partnership needs development support to go *beyond structure.* In addition to the usual boards/executives/forums that get established at the outset, the LSP needs to develop the local detail of everyday work, to do with strengthening partnership work *and* delivering desired outcomes. These multiple activities that will in due course criss-cross as well as extend well beyond the formal structure cannot be presupposed by an organogram. *Things like creating meeting agendas, engaging partner organizations, linking one level of meeting to another, following up project plans, and so on (and their form, frequency, and relational nature)* need to be created through specific interactions between specific people at specific times.

» One way of characterizing this net of complex, criss-crossing communications and relations is to liken it to a largely invisible fabric that links everything together in a systemic way. By its very nature, this *infrastructure* needs to be woven or stitched together piece by piece through the many events of everyday local action—for example, *following up the sending out of meeting minutes with a phone call to a key colleague to identify and agree interim steps; or, meeting with colleagues in your own organization to explain and explore the implications of supporting particular projects being pursued by the LSP.* It is these that bring vibrant life (or, through their lack, lead to a sense of malaise) to the formal structures put in place initially and (to mix metaphors) build operational flesh on the strategic skeleton.

» This stitching-together-of-infrastructure through doing things together is largely a *tacit* process (Polanyi, 1983): in getting on with the everyday issues of making the partnership work, partners are also creating (or not creating) a dynamic network of relations. This "getting on" is something that by its very nature has to be done by the actual members of the LSP, and so it is a *group* process. It is only through this working together that local know-how can be accessed, the requisite relations crafted, and the quality of joint commitment enhanced. This is not something that can be designed or instructed from on high by specialists or those in the chairing roles. If this is not done, people only "do" partnership work at the meetings, and the necessary dynamic of new thinking followed by experimentation, and by learning between meetings, fails to develop. *An important learning in this LSP was that no communications were taking place between the Board chair and his "rotating" Executive chairs, after Board meetings or prior to Executive meetings, with the result that little focus or momentum was being developed.*

» Given the novelty and uncertainty of the LSP form of local governance, this "stitching infrastructure" process has in many ways to be a creative and artistic process as people feel and fashion their way forward—for example, how can we go on in our "place-shaping" role? Though there is high-level guidance from government, these new organizations by their nature have to be largely one-off inventions that connect with the local scene in unique ways. So again using Lyotard (1984), the LSP cannot work within existing "rules". Instead, by creating a partnership that learns to exist and deliver a useful service successfully in its local context, they will in fact have created the new rules of effective leadership in partnership *in what will have been done. So in this LSP the development of "cross-cutting initiatives" was shown to offer a new way of using limited funding to make progress on a number of strategic fronts*

» By inference, successful work in this context will not be just *ideas* about success, but *actual* success. In other words, the successful future the group might imagine will also need to have been "presenced" (Scharmer, 2006), with the partners embodying in present behaviour as they work together the quality of relationships and lived values that are the essence of that future. *What became very clear during the development meetings was the cumulative power of several successful open and frank debates between local-authority and third-sector partners in raising the level of between-meeting activity and initiatives aimed at improving collaboration.*

» Developing leadership in partnership (and by definition in these peer groups, *all* members are potentially leaders) therefore requires partners to find ways of working successfully on the business issues and then reflexively identifying what it was that "worked well" and "what supported what worked well" (Cooperrider & Avital, 2004). In other words partners need also to *capture the development process* as they learn to work effectively and then use this knowledge to help others in their wider network develop the effectiveness of the partnership at large. *One example of this was the development of a "strategic storyline" for each of the cross-cutting projects. This process helped members of the Executive educate themselves about the "why/what/ how" aspects of the projects and provided strong grounds for crafting the funding proposals to the Board.*

We may call this overall process one that addresses the challenge of *systemic presencing:* helping a group embody in present behaviour the essence of new ways of behaving in partnership that take account of the social and political realities these desired new patterns have to measure up to. It feels to us that CLM, with its dual focus on performing *and* developing, is well adapted to support/ accelerate this kind of natural development process possessed by self-determining systems.

Conclusions

This has been an unusual and most enlightening project for us. By dint of resisting initial demands for a structured and clear-cut approach, and by responding to the particular exigencies of client availability, we have found it possible to adopt a more open-ended and *mutual* approach to our work with the client. Instead of trying to lead the client as expected, we have been able to engage with them in a struggle to try to understand what an appropriate role for the LSP might be and how they might best use their resources to achieve this. In adopting this more "side-by-side" role, we have become much more aware of important difficulties a more organized approach can cover or skate over, for both client and consultant. We have been shown how fruitful and generative a more self-effacing approach can be.

However, going down this mutual inquiry route is not without its difficulties and downsides. Despite effective development events, busy clients found it difficult to take up the active roles required, and many did not get involved in follow-up activities between meetings. Furthermore, there was a lack of formality concerning individual responsibility towards the process. Due to the emergent nature of the process, no such "learning contract" was agreed, and this made us quite tentative in one-to-one follow-up work. When follow-up e-mail notes, proposals, and questions were met with a blank silence, we found it difficult to sense where the process was heading. The consequent feeling of disengagement and loss of momentum on both sides did lead to people doubting that much was different, as well as to concerns about committing more time and energy to the difficulties facing the development process. During such times, we as co-inquirers needed to walk a tricky path, with some parties pushing us towards becoming more interventionist and "teachy", while our own experience suggested we needed to be careful not to act in ways that would cover up weaknesses "in the system". What helped us deal with these siren-like recidivist temptations was to keep reminding ourselves that the LSP itself had to learn to become self-sustaining—and that our bright ideas would probably be a distraction to what really needed to be done.

Nevertheless, this experience can offer ideas to the systemic consultant and developer in terms of engagement, focus, and role, in reducing the "transfer gap" mentioned at the outset. For instance, it is evident that attention to questions of *intention* and *context* are vital: these are often taken for granted and are difficult to raise once a process has started. With our MA students, it can take some time for them to frame the MA as *part* of their own development trajectory, rather than an end in itself, and consequently how important it is for them to take charge of developing their own tacit knowledge. Similarly with members of the LSP, it seemed to require them both to realize afresh why they "signed up" and to recognize their personal responsibility for what was happening—that what might happen in the future is very much in their hands—before the process really engaged them.

In both situations the particular role taken by the coach seems quite critical in bringing closer the performing and developing aspects of work. "De-centring" one's power (White, 1997) to allow mutual inquiry to take place in an emergent fashion has seemed to free up the thinking and behaviour of both individuals and groups. Furthermore, applying design tools like the "development sandwich" to enrich the learning-while-working experience, and using some form of systemic thinking to offer contrasting ways of seeing/feeling situations and interactions, also seem to have reinforced the sense of "liberation with responsibility" that comes from knowing they have choice in how they see and respond to situations.

The aim in all this has been to close the gap between performing and developing by creating dynamic learning architectures for this kind of *both* performance *and* development at the same time. Though this is still very much in embryo, the results we have been getting are encouraging us to work with both students and clients in a more intuitive and improvisatory way, creating unique working/learning opportunities to improve leadership in the system.

Notes

1. Batteau, Gosling, and Mintzberg (2006) define "close learning" as follows: "We refer to this design as 'close learning' because it is close in time and place to where the work gets done, the participants' leadership practice . . . close learning is concerned with knowledge that exists primarily in the mind–body relationships of the learner. It is created and displayed in the way things get done—and in what gets done. As thinking changes, these practices change and more aspects come into focus. It is a process of discovery and, in essence, mastery, rather than one of explanation" (p. 8).

2. It is worth spending a bit of time unpacking what this idea of closeness or nearness might mean. In Batteau, Gosling, and Mintzberg's work (2006), the term initially came up in the context of distance learning, but now I think the use is more to do with the focus being on practice rather

than education per se; it also appears to mean bringing experience to the classroom so learning there can be transferred more easily to the workplace. What is more interesting is the notion that it needs to/will also influence not only the individual but the workplace too. So we get the idea that the learning is not just about the isolated individual. I would like to make this more obvious: "close learning" is not only about influencing individual practice but about influencing the relational and social dimension, the context, in which these improvements in practice might take place—that is, changed practice requires support from those around it and the norms/power disciplines that legitimate certain claims to truth and marginalize others. So we are talking about more than individual learning here and are starting to move towards ideas of communities of practice (Wenger,1998) who learn together, much of it at an implicit or tacit level. I would also like to dynamize the idea further and propose that "closeness" goes even further to take account of the process and complexity theory assumptions—that is, that the future is constructed in a fleeting present moment, against a complex and continuously changing social/political background process. So we are not talking just about situated learning being brought closer to the domain of practice but that this situated learning is embedded in a higher-level learning process that enables participants to continuously update and re-contextualize that learning in the light of emergence. Without this, any learning is almost immediately de-contextualized and outdated. This brings to mind what Torbert (2004) has called "triple-loop learning" and what Bateson in an earlier age referred to as processes associated with "second/deutero learning" and possibly "third-level learning" (Bateson, 1972).

CHAPTER FOUR

Locating conflict in team consultations

David Campbell

Commentary

In the next two chapters, by David Campbell and by Marianne Grønbæk, respectively, we return to consultation with teams and an approach to working with teams with difficulties in relating to one another that is based on a recent development in dialogical theory. David Campbell is interested in facilitating work groups to speak and listen to each other in a dialogical manner.

Positioning theory suggests that our sense of self and the other in an organization or elsewhere is the result of taking a position or being positioned by others on a continuum that consists of many possible positions and meanings for oneself and the other. These positions are provisional and not fixed, yet teams can behave as if they are, and this can lead to insoluble conflicts and the lack of safety to discuss and resolve them. Campbell's innovative work with people in teams focuses on trying to help them step back from themselves and get a bit of distance from the positions they have taken up or been placed in.

He describes the mindset he takes into a team consultation and how he frames this for the team in a didactic manner so as to create a different kind of space in which they might have a dialogue with one another. When he thinks he has identified a tension or conflict in the team, he attempts to articulate it and share with the team his idea of the continuum along which members of the team have taken positions. This is what is meant by a semantic polarity. The naming of the continuum and the poles at either end allow people to identify a variety of views and in particular to express different and unorthodox views. This is the basis for creative solutions to emerge out of dialogical conversations, sometimes about highly contentious issues. In this respect, this consultation method could be seen as a technique for mediation and conflict resolution that is very different from traditional approaches. These usually seek to explicate the established sides in a conflict, rather than start the interaction from a totally different place where the parties can join in a dialogue, as Campbell's approach does.

The semantic polarity method clearly has a lot of potential for stuck long-standing public sector and human service teams where the patterns of interaction can become overly fixed, perhaps because of the difficult clients they work with or the external organizational uncertainties they constantly face. It would be interesting to see how Campbell would adapt the approach to more aggressively business-focused private sector teams where difference seems easier to express, perhaps even exaggerated, because of the openness to the external competitive environment and the relative clarity of the profit-making task.   [Eds.]

The model I am presenting in this chapter represents one particular branch of the great, amorphous body of ideas called systemic thinking—that is, the recent development in dialogical theory. Whereas systemic practitioners have long been interested in the interaction and observable feedback loops between parts of the system, it is more recently that the field has begun to theorize about the way meanings are created in a dialogical process (Bertrando, 2007; Seikkula & Arnkil, 2006)). As a consultant I am interested in facilitating teams and small services to speak and listen to each other in a dialogical manner, rather than imposing my own formulation of team dynamics as though a new understanding of dynamics is sufficient to create new conversations. And I have been searching for ideas and models to help me facilitate these conversations.

What is emerging for me is a combination of ideas from three or four theoretical strands that I am putting together in my current work. In this chapter, I describe the central ideas and offer a few case examples to show how I am putting them to use. If readers want to take these ideas further, they are also spelt out with 14 case examples in a recent book, *Taking Positions in the Organization* (Campbell & Grønbæk, 2006).

Fundamental concepts

The model is based on four central assumptions:

1. The conflicts and obstacles presented by clients, or gleaned by the consultant, signify the areas that must be addressed in some way before a team can move forward.
2. Particular people within a team need to feel free and safe to address these issues before change can happen.
3. The best new ideas will emerge from a conversation among the appropriate people who are able to listen to and be influenced by other people's ideas. This is the basis for a dialogical model for addressing conflict.
4. Once a person's position is acknowledged and valued, he or she can loosen his or her grip on that position and begin looking around for new ideas and positions that will facilitate his or her own development.

Positioning theory, as proposed by Harré and Langenhove (1999), suggests that our sense of self and of "the other" is the result of taking a position or being positioned by others on a continuum that consists of many possible positions and many possible meanings for self and other. For example, if I grow up believing I am a person unworthy of respect, this means that someone, somewhere, has evaluated me on the continuum called "worthy of respect", looked me over, and then positioned me at the far end of this continuum as: "someone unworthy of love" (as opposed to a position at the other end of the continuum: someone "very worthy of respect"). But this represents one position among many possible positions on the continuum, so the "positioner", perhaps a parent or a work colleague, must have some notion of what a person *unworthy* of respect is in order to place me further along the continuum as a person *worthy* of respect. This is an example of *being positioned* by others. Similarly, if I believe I am a person unworthy of respect, this becomes a position I choose on a similar continuum, which is an example of *taking a position*. The following diagram makes the point that we are both positioned and taking positions in our organizations, but our concept of "who we are" in the organization then results, fundamentally, from an interplay and comparison between different positions that results in one position being assigned or chosen:

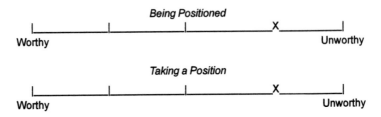

The meaning we attach to these positions is the result of looking around and comparing our position to other positions not taken, or not offered. On this basis, we know we are in a strong position only when we have some experience of a weak position and have some sense of the difference between the two.

The Russian literary critic Bakhtin (1981), the psychologist Sampson (1993), and others since have spoken about the way we create meaning through language by offering words to other people to be confirmed. We try out a word or a sentence in order to have a confirmation of a meaning we have in mind. Meaning comes from others, or, more precisely, it comes from the interplay between people. We offer ourselves in conversation hoping that the response will give us a meaning and a direction for what to do next, or to tell us, as Wittgenstein put it, "how to go on".

Another helpful idea here is that the position we take or are given by others is momentary. The relationships we are in are constantly changing and creating the possibility of new meanings moment by moment. Therefore, if we choose a position on one continuum or in one context, we can also choose a different position on a new continuum of possible meanings.

Doing the consultation

When I work with teams or organizations, I often try to get people interested in these ideas because the process is non-blaming and enables people to feel safe enough to explore the difficult issues and problems they bring to a consultation. I often say to them, "let's imagine that everything we say here is merely a position, and the position you take is a platform from which you can connect up with other people who have other positions but who give value and meaning to you by responding explicitly or implicitly to your position".

This way of thinking has the effect of letting people step back from themselves and get a bit of distance from their own thoughts and feelings. This helps them appreciate that they are in the midst of a continuous and active process of finding meanings and defining themselves by choosing a position in the midst of many other possible positions.

And I find if I persist with clients, and do not give up at the first look of bafflement, many people find the ideas are freeing. It allows for new perspectives that re-contextualize the problem as it is seen by the client. *Any* form of process consultation relies on the ability to help people get some distance from their own thoughts and actions and see things in the wider context. The crucial point here is that I am trying to place people on a continuum in which they are part of a momentary relationship that is creating meanings; and if meanings are being created in *this* moment, the conversational process also has the potential to create new, non-dysfunctional meanings in the *next* moment or to remove the obstacles so clients can use the functional abilities they already have. I shall say more about this below.

In order to help a team listen and speak in a dialogical manner, I need to begin by enabling people to feel safe in the presence of others. This is a big challenge for consultants who work with groups because, unlike a one-to-one relationship such as a coaching session, the members of a team or organization will be speaking in public, and they may be vulnerable to misunderstandings, malign interpretations, projections, and attack from the others in the room, and whether or not this happens, many clients will be in a self-protective or defensive stance as they present themselves in a consultation session. Work teams and organizations are places where behaviour is repetitive and can be seen as falling into a pattern. It is not long before colleagues' behaviour is predictable. I heard one person say recently, "I know what my colleague is going to say before she opens her mouth". And when it is predictable, it becomes associated with that person and becomes a "personal style" or a "personal quality". When behaviour is equated with the person, it can be absorbed as part of the "self" and soon feel like an internal state or character trait, and it is therefore much more difficult to get the proper distance to see alternatives and much more difficult to change.

So, my assumption on first sitting down with a group is that each individual is to some extent protecting him/herself. I acknowledge this may be the case and that it is important for people to take this position, but I also want to invite them to think of the group process differently; therefore, I introduce the notion that the qualities they see in others are not about the person but are merely positions taken by that person on a particular continuum. I do this in a fairly didactic, "teacherly" manner, and I usually make an example from the next comment or question from the group by saying, "You have just taken a position with that comment, let's step back and put your statement on a continuum and consider other possible positions that there might be on this continuum."

Case example 1

For example, I recently began a consultation to a HR department in a medium-sized manufacturing company that asked for help to unify the vision and direction of the department. When I began, I could feel tension and resistance to my presence in the room. I started by telling the group of about ten people that whether they were evaluating this as a good consultation or a bad one depended on an interplay of many different perspectives, from "this consultation is a great idea" at one end to "this consultation is a terrible idea" at the other end, but the important point is that the most valid evaluation of this consultation experience emerges from a dialogical process among the different positions. Then I drew the two polarities on a line and asked each person to come up to the flip chart, take the felt-tip marker and indicate their position on this continuum, so we could see the different positions we had available to begin the dialogue from. Nine of them duly placed marks on the line between the poles, but one placed his mark at the top of the paper about 6 inches above the line, indicating that he was strongly against the idea of the consultation, nor did he want to take part in the exercise:

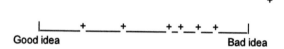

However, this gave us the opportunity to discuss themes such as, "what did it mean that people would attend something they felt so strongly against?" and "how could the consultation itself address very different expectations?" and "what kind of status do such 'outlying' positions have in the organization—for if he is an outlier on this continuum, perhaps others are outliers on other continua?"

Case example 2

Because the positions and polarity lines are visual, they can make an impact when words and ideas have become neutralized. For example, I was recently consulting to a Child and Adolescent Mental Health (CAMHS) team that felt very unsupported by their service manager, Michael. The group presented a long catalogue of complaints about Michael, and one worker in particular expressed his grievance, saying things like: "he doesn't have a clue what we are trying to do" and "he is not managing us and should be brought to book". As we talked, I could not shift his thinking to see a broader, more systemic perspective, but it then occurred to me to draw a polarity line with two positions representing the CAMHS worker on one side and Michael on the other, like this:

And I called this polarity:

"Perspectives on Management"

The visual representation seemed to help the CAMHS worker literally see that his point of view was only one position, and it helped him become more curious about Michael as also having a valid position—even on the same polarity line! From this we went on to discuss the different context within which Michael could be seen to be doing his job, and, as examples, the group generated ideas about how he managed his budget and how he protected his seniors from criticism.

Within this model, I assume every organization needs some form of ongoing dialogue between orthodoxy and unorthodoxy in order to define and develop its central purpose, and therefore it is crucial that unorthodoxy is given a position. If the person who habitually speaks out about the "emperor's new clothes" drifts too far from the centre and leaves the organization, the position of unorthodoxy will be assigned to someone else. And I often discuss this organizational process with the participants of a consultation.

I have found over the years that all of these things—the theoretical model and the open discussion—contribute to a climate in which participants feel that whatever difficulties the organization may be going through is less about the person and more about the position. By framing the personal as an organizational process, it reduces personal blame for the situation. This allows people to feel less self-protective about their behaviour, safer, and therefore more open to being influenced by new ideas from other people and other positions.

Using the dialogical model

I now want to move to the next stage of my consultation model. This assumes that work has been done and a group are now feeling sufficiently safe to re-examine their own ideas and assumptions about others and the organization.

The final part of the model I am using is based on dialogical theory. Many writers and clinicians have contributed to the development of this field, from philosophers such as Martin Buber (1970), to social constructionists such as Kenneth Gergen (1994) and John Shotter (1993), and on to Mikhail Bakhtin (1981) and the Finnish psychologist, Jaakko Seikkula (Seikkula & Arnkil, 2006).

What I have borrowed from this field is the notion that new ideas emerge from dialogue, which depends on the ability of each partner to be influenced by the ideas and the presence of the other. In order to be influenced, we have to feel secure enough to entertain the notion that we may change our position by listening to people from other positions. As part of the consultation process, I often lead a team towards a process in which they can have dialogical conversations with each other about issues that are highly contentious. I begin the process by identifying different positions held by team members and, crucially, explain my conviction that we need the positions of others to hold our own positions. When people get interested and curious about the idea of the interdependence of different positions, and when this can be done in a non-blaming atmosphere, they begin to risk, metaphorically, lifting their heads, looking around at other positions, and taking an interest.

Dialogue between two people on different positions does not just happen. It has to be orchestrated. And often it has to be monitored by an observer or myself. The natural tendency when people begin to speak is to defend their position by trying to convince the other about the "rightness" of their own position; this sends messages to the other that the discussion is about persuasion rather than listening, and, as a result, the recipient prepares to defend his or her own position against an onslaught of persuasion. A dialogue between two people needs a measure of motivation, goodwill, and desire to try something new. Many people have written about the ground rules that facilitate dialogue (Becker, Chasin,

Chasin, Herig, & Routh, 1995; Penman, 1992); I will not review all of them here, but I do want to share the question I currently use and have found most helpful to begin the process. When two or more people are in place and ready to begin, I ask them to take it in turns to speak to each other to learn about the other's experience, and their position for this particular issue, and this can be guided by answering the following question:

> "WHY IS IT, PERSONALLY, SO IMPORTANT FOR THE OTHER
> TO TAKE THEIR POSITION?"

I think there are several reasons why this question works. First, it is not about the validity of the position statement itself. For example, in a team discussion, this would not be about the merits of a type of service nor about the best use of resources. It is about what lies behind the position.

If, as in the diagram below, there are two positions about management (should be less directive, should be more directive), this question does not address the validity of a management style per se; rather, it addresses the value and meaning of the other taking that particular position. Second, it allows people to speak person-ally. It allows them to bring a different aspect of their position to light that has probably not been acknowledged because the positions have been debated on the basis of evidence or cost. This question allows people to go behind the position (represented by the triangles), and, by listening to a personal statement, the urge to persuade and the urge to defend are diminished. I find that per-sonal statements such as this are not threatening, and this allows the other to listen more openly; when this happens, the listener is more receptive to another colleague but, more importantly, is receptive to the merits of another position. It happens occasionally

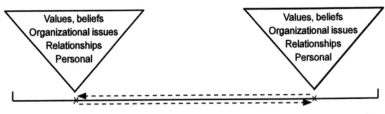

management should be less directive   management should be more directive

that people find this is a difficult conversation to have and revert to arguing the correctness of their position, and I have to tell them that that is a different conversation. We may need to have the conversation about correctness, but if we can have this one first, they will hear more that is said in the subsequent conversation.

This is the theory, but how does it work in practice? In "real-life" consultations I have found it is most difficult to find the theme or issue or what I call the "polarity line" that people are able to have a dialogue about. Dialogue will not happen until both parties feel they are, metaphorically, on a level playing field. It cannot be skewed in any way—for example, if one is speaking from a position of greater power, or if one is dragged to the conversation, or if one is seen as occupying a negative position, or if one feels sorry for the other. These types of conversations are probably necessary in organizational life, but they are not dialogical. I have found that dialogue only takes place when two or more people are equally interested in listening to the other with an open mind—that is, that they each feel they have something to gain by coming together.

I have found that the implication of this is profound. It means that the biggest challenge facing the consultant is finding the theme or polarity that links everyone and places them, metaphorically, on a level playing field. At this point some readers may be thinking that this aspect of the work is akin to making an interpretation to a family or group that embraces all participants equally, and I would agree the process is very similar, but with one important difference—as I search my mind for a suitable theme, or polarity, I am asking myself: in what areas are these people looking for some new ideas from the others in the room? Not the areas that I or others might hope they would like to discuss, but themes that people in antagonistic positions would genuinely like to discuss, for their own benefit. This takes the consultant back to the basic assumption that when our positions are acknowledged and appreciated, we will begin to look for new positions to support our development. To help me find the theme people will engage in, I have developed my own mantra that runs like this:

"WHAT DO THESE PEOPLE, *REALLY*, WANT TO LISTEN TO THAT COMES FROM A POSITION OTHER THAN THEIR OWN?"

And I keep chipping away at this question until I have found the theme that joins the pair or group, and that becomes the topic to begin the dialogue. Finding the theme is a delicate interplay between the themes I think may be helpful, based on my hypotheses about the organization or dynamics I have observed on the one hand, and the themes that the group are keen to discuss on the other. I will often be suggesting certain themes, but I give precedence to what a group is willing and able to discuss, because I am using a dialogical model, not a group dynamic model. This means I prioritize the facilitation of dialogue—any dialogue, to get things going—rather than assuming that there are certain things that must be addressed. If I can get one dialogical conversation off the ground, the participants will have a new experience and then feel more confident about applying this method to other, more challenging themes.

You might imagine, for example, that it would be impossible to have a dialogue in a climate in which there are unspoken differences of power, as is often the case in troubled organizations. And I assume it may be impossible for an employee to have a "dialogical" conversation with his boss; nevertheless, if I were using the dialogical model, I would search for the issues that lie behind the struggle for power such as status and respect, career advancement, or feelings of insecurity. If such themes become apparent to me, I might try to establish conversations in which the whole team would share their ideas and feelings about the best way to "manage career advancement" in a small, competitive organization. It is a jointly acknowledged theme such as this that brings people together, and then it is the question—"*Why is it so important, personally, for the other to take their position?*"—that begins the dialogue.

Case example 3

One thing that is generally difficult to deal with in teams is the feeling of exclusion. I have observed that when teams avoid the topic, some people will feel further excluded because they think they are alone with their feelings. I recently consulted to an NHS team that provided psychological services to a wide and remote geographical area that meant they had only themselves to turn to for support, and I hypothesized that this might make differences harder to acknowledge. After a few hours with this group, I asked them to move around the room silently and place themselves in a physical configuration that represented their relationships to each other. (Incidentally this can be a very powerful intervention that releases emotion and allows people to express things they may not be able to convey with words. Because it is public, everyone takes a position but is simultaneously positioned by others. It can be seen as a physical manifestation of the positioning work I described above.)

This sculpting exercise immediately revealed that several people were clustered together and several others were alone on the periphery. This was particularly upsetting to one woman on the edge, as it aroused her feeling of being excluded by the team. After we sat down and talked about the feelings this aroused, I decided to use the positioning model to illustrate the way every organization must create a range of positions to have diversity, but if, as in this case, there is a value to cluster together, like a central tendency, then the central cluster may also need the presence of outliers, like the woman in the sculpt, who actually define the central people by being peripheral people. It is as though people could say: "I know I belong because I can identify someone who does not belong."

I represented this with the following diagram:

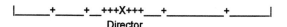

Director

With this diagram on a flip chart, I asked the group to get into pairs to discuss two things: first, why it was important to take the position they chose within the sculpt? I asked them to discuss this because I wanted to challenge the feeling of being victimized and emphasize their own initiative in choosing where to stand. I think this enabled the woman on the periphery to reflect on how this is a long-standing pattern for her of struggling to feel included in groups, but also she was quite comfortable being on the edge.

Then, because the issue about the way the director seemed to manage by emphasizing closeness, perhaps at the expense of difference, was in the back of my mind, I asked these pairs to work together to produce two polarity lines for each of them: one line on which they were in the centre of things and fully included, and another on which they were on the edge of things and in danger of feeling excluded. The point I want to highlight here is that the emphasis was not on choosing a position, because I was prescribing that they position themselves in the middle and on the edge; rather, the emphasis was on giving a name to the issue, or context, or polarity line that dictated the position they took. So, for example, the woman on the periphery of the sculpt made two lines. The first was the one in which she was on the edge and she called it this:

"Feeling I am respected by the director"

Then she presented her second polarity line in which she was central and the director was some distance from her, and this polarity she labelled:

"Feeling committed to my model of work with clients"

When each person had had this chance to think about the way he or she positioned others on the periphery, and him/herself in the centre, I asked the staff members to change the pairings and to go off with someone for whom there was disagreement or conflict about how they saw each other's position, and to get together to learn, as in the previous diagram, what lay behind the positions they were given or the positions they chose. I felt that the fact they had done some prior work to see their behaviour as an important part of an organizational process made it easier in the second phase to face the people they were in conflict with.

Using polarities in the "middle ground"

Positioning theory and the semantic polarities model can be used at many levels of application. At the least formal, structural level, they represent a range of ideas anyone can keep in mind while at work. For example, any of us, while listening to a colleague in a meeting, can appreciate that statements and questions are merely positions and they have the effect of positioning others and limiting their options for thinking and acting in the organization. At the other extreme, this model can be used to establish the grounds for dialogical conversations among work colleagues, particularly those who have been positioned in opposition to each other.

And then there are the applications of the model between these extremes. In this territory, a consultant can infuse his or her organizational thinking and offer formulations to clients that reflect the positioning going on in the organization and provide the basis for new conversations. It is this middle ground that I want to illustrate with the following case example. (Readers who want further examples of the application of this model are referred to chapter 5, as well as to Campbell & Grønbæk, 2006.)

Case example 4

I was asked to consult to a multidisciplinary team of 12 practitioners who had responsibility for providing therapeutic services for young people, supervision of other professionals, and support for foster and adoptive parents within a local area.

The team had been formed a few years earlier by bringing staff together from other existing services, and there had been many struggles for the team to work well together and to define their overlapping relationships with other local services. Their current concern, when I was asked to help, was that one of the team members had made a formal complaint against two others for a form of verbal bullying. While the investigation was going on, the staff were prevented from speaking about the matter.

I only knew this much when I arrived to meet the whole team, but I could sense the manager preferred not to tell me the details of the complaint because she wanted me to be able to remain neutral and not be seen to take sides within the team dynamics. It seemed to me she wanted to "not make things worse" since a conclusion to the complaint had been reached, and the staff wanted to try to move on with their work. So, as I drank my coffee and the individuals arrived to start the consultation, I was trying to think of a way I could respect the manager's wishes but, at the same time, enable the team to explore the fraught and complex feelings that, I surmised, must be associated with the recent complaint.

When we began the meeting, I asked them what issues were important for them to discuss in this particular setting. There were strong feelings directed at the managers, such as senior managers and HR staff, for the way the whole complaint episode had been handled. I was keenly aware of the absence of any expressed feeling directed towards anyone in the team, and at this stage I was not aware of who had made the complaint against whom. I felt a tremendous collective desire not to stir things up and make people more wounded than they already were. I knew I had been contracted to meet this group four times, and I decided not to question this situation directly, but to assume that this represented the manner in which the group felt they could best recover from the trauma of the complaint investigation and get on with working as a service team. It seemed to me there was a lot that was not being addressed, but that it may be more accessible at a later time.

Therefore, I decided to create an opportunity for them to voice their complaints about management and, at the same time, create a story about the event that allowed some of the more difficult feelings to be expressed. I went to the flip chart and drew a polarity line with "It is wrong" at one end and "It is understandable" at the other:

| |_____| |
It is wrong   It is understandable

By choosing to polarize these statements, I wanted to convey that the group's recovery could be represented by movement back and forth between the expression of their feelings, at one end, and the understanding of the process, at the other. I thought there was a danger they might get stuck in an outpouring of feeling that confirmed they were the victims of poor management. So, by placing this position on a polarity line indicating a relationship with processing and understanding the experience, the group were given clear messages that they could move when they were ready and they could also return to further expression of their feelings when that was necessary. One could argue that this approach avoids the direct discussion of the feelings within the group, but my judgment at the time was that the group were not ready for this, nor was I, as I had just met the group and was still feeling my way.

During the ensuing discussion and subsequent coffee break, I was asking myself, "how could a group get to such a state that differences could not be discussed before they had escalated into serious communication problems and a formal complaint?" and I was questioning how I could provide a safe context for the group to discuss this. I came up with the idea that the group had polarized around the need to respect privacy and difference at one pole, and a need to share a common approach to the work and emphasize similarities, at the other. So, I discussed this with the group and put the following polarity on the flip chart:

|_____|

The need for a   The need to respect
shared story   individuals' privacy

This polarity led to a discussion about why there was so much emphasis on consensual decision-making and keeping everyone in the team involved and happy. I tried to represent the opposite position by suggesting that too much emphasis on "teamness" will position some individuals as being outside the acceptable team culture and therefore easy targets for blame or scapegoating, and when blame gets into a team culture, it is very difficult to maintain open, dialogical conversations. I then asked what pressures from outside the team might contribute to a blame culture, and they said they felt "set up" by the wider professional network to come in as the experts and sort out messy cases that everyone struggled with, but the team couldn't meet the expectations of the outside world. In this discussion one member said something that struck me forcibly and made an impact on my thinking. She said, "There is no compassion from the kids to their carers." This one comment led me to develop another hypothesis that linked the discussion about blaming each other to the issue of compassion.

I wanted to play with the idea that a lack of compassion may also be reflected in staff relations, thus adding to the blame culture the group described. Again, my aim was to introduce this theme in a way that it could be discussed and team members could experience how they might move back and forth from positions that are uncomfortable to positions less so. I went to the flip chart once more and drew the following polarity line:

```
|_____|
Compassion for self                    Compassion for others
```

Based on the staff member's statement, "There is no compassion from the kids to their carers", it would not have been helpful to let "the kids" or the team members get identified with a negative position such as "not showing compassion", because that would make it less likely that the group would explore the value and meaning of that position. Therefore it was important for stimulating a conversation that the polarity was named in terms that were positive and that allowed the group to get interested in the positions and why the children or indeed the staff would take such a position. (As was discussed earlier in the chapter, this model strives to convert behavioural or character traits such as "lacking compassion" into positions on semantic polarity lines, because this process is less blaming, and therefore people are more likely to be curious about a position they see having some positive attributes.) With this polarity, named in this way, the children who did not show compassion to staff could be seen as looking after themselves, not others, and perhaps the staff, under the stress from the outside world, were also looking after themselves and not the others on the team.

In the course of 2½ hours of discussion during this consultation, these polarity lines were produced, and drawn on flip charts, as a result of the ideas that emerged in the discussion. I was actively trying to gather important themes and polarize them to validate different points of view and stretch the boundaries of what was acceptable to talk about. But at the same time I saw myself as a very active organizer of the discussion, selecting the themes, polarizing them in particular ways, and making graphic representations on flip charts. The flip-chart pages remained on the walls throughout the discussion, as reminders of the polarities we had developed, and could be returned to when needed at any time in the discussion. For me, they were a visual, fixed depiction of important themes, but also a reminder to all of us that we were merely discussing positions and therefore they could be changed from one discussion to the next.

Conclusion

So, what kinds of tools can the consultant take away from the work I have presented here? As a consultant working with a group, I find it very challenging, to say the least, to try to keep track of the themes that emerge and overlap as the discussion unfolds; and I find the use of the polarity lines on flip charts helps me keep track of themes, and keeps the themes in the group consciousness. I think I am also creating a dynamic tension in the group between the stated and explicit position within a theme and the possibility of many positions that can be chosen by the participants themselves.

One message that I hope comes across to the reader is that the ideas and techniques of positioning theory, semantic polarities, and dialogical conversation may have been presented here as a loose model for consultation, but they are best used as specific tools that help the consultant reframe consultation as an opportunity to create process, not just to observe it or to interpret it. The consultant can redefine process consultation as something more active and dynamic between the consultant and his or her clients. The tools, or ways of seeing process, allow the consultant to orchestrate new, highly focused conversations that, at the same time, encourage flexibility and movement to new positions. Finally, although sharing some common features, this is not a model for conflict resolution, nor is the aim that team members from different positions will compromise and move to the middle ground. Rather, this is a model that enables people to be genuinely influenced, through safer dialogic conversations, by the ideas or experiences that have been located in positions other than their own.

CHAPTER FIVE

The power of keeping it simple

Marianne Grønbæk

Commentary

In the second chapter devoted to working with positioning theory, Marianne Grønbæk describes how she uses semantic polarities in her consultation work with both public and private sector organizations. After an explanation of what semantic polarities are and how they can help people feel safe and able to tackle sensitive and potentially conflictual discussions, she describes her "Growth Model" as an addition to this. It is a model for having difficult conversations and is based on appreciative inquiry (Hammond, 1996). Grønbæk noticed that, in traditional problem-solving, the drive is to find solutions and that many important conversations about a situation get missed, particularly those about challenges and possibilities. The Growth Model involves creating a platform for work with clients in a consultation that allows these creative possibilities to emerge so as to enrich the dialogue and enhance decision-making.

Grønbæk applies semantic polarities and the Growth Model to her consultation work with a school where the managers wanted the staff to manage meetings and decision-making more effectively. She takes the reader through the negotiation of the work with the school Principal and two managers to the design of the day's consultation and then how this was implemented, interspersing her account with the reflections that guided her work at each stage.

A critical point that emerges from this chapter is the care that must be taken in choosing the semantic polarities, some of which can be worked out before a consultation as part of contracting conversations with the client and some of which need to be developed in the moment. Perhaps clients also come up with suggestions of their own.

This brings us to another key point of interest in this chapter, of the way Grønbæk describes giving the clients tools for having future safe conversations with one another. The giving of tools represents a difference between this kind of systemic consultation and traditional process consultation, where clients would not usually be given tools and techniques for working by the consultant. This is because it could represent the consultant as expert rather than the client and might mean that the consultant was taking control of the process rather than observing and commenting upon the client's process. In this case, it could be argued that the consultant gives tools and techniques that help the client to manage their own process and decision-making more effectively, rather than taking away control and managing it for them towards a predetermined outcome.

Grønbæk's chapter presents fun, interesting, and in-depth ways to work with clients who want to have different conversations with one another; however, although she says this helps with difficult conversations, her case example does not really show how clients who are really stuck and in tension and distress would use the tools she describes to help them. It would be interesting to see how the ideas would work in a case where feelings are running much higher and there is less goodwill and willingness to work together. [Eds.]

I am very interested in the idea that we have to be in a dialogue in order to develop new thoughts about relationships and the way we act and react with each other. I like the idea of how we get influenced by other people's thoughts, and the various ways we influence each other.

When working with positioning theory and semantic polarities, it seems very important both to oneself and to others to consider the position *you* think you are talking from, the position others think you are talking from, and the positions you think other people are listening from. In my consultation work, I embrace the idea that "every statement is just a position". I have been fascinated by how easy a consultation can be, yet, on the other hand, my clients experienced the conversations as "deep" and as bringing change in the way people were thinking about the issues in question and about each other. Working with semantic polarities and positions stimulates my wish to be in a constant process of developing new and more helpful conversations and understandings. My philosophy as a consultant is that all organizations, groups, families are different. The consultant is to be the curious guest in their world. So even if I think I have a conversation model that I can use in order to be a good consultant, I have to be an open-minded guest coming into their organization, and I have to transform the models into something clients can use in order to make progress that they will be proud of.

It is all about positions—and I think we have to be aware of the positions we take as consultants.

In this chapter, I focus on semantic polarities and positions and the Growth Model as the ideas that relate to the case study I have chosen.

The following is a short presentation of the thoughts behind semantic polarities and the Growth Model, and I hope that, together with the case study, they will give a sufficient impression—enough for the reader to understand and perhaps become inspired to use some of the ideas.

A short presentation of the thoughts behind semantic polarities and positions

Semantic polarity thinking is based on the thought that it is important for people to be in a safe context when they are talking about changes. Whatever we say is to be seen and heard as "a position" from which we can be speaking and be heard. You can read more about the model in *Taking Positions in the Organization* (Campbell & Grønbæk, 2006).

The following four statements seem to provide a framework for talking about polarities and positions:

"It is just a position."

"The way we choose to see the world creates the world we see."

"Thoughts, language, actions, habits, and character are connected."

"Changing one of them will influence the others".

People are always influenced by the situation and the relations they are part of. Whatever we think, say, or do can be seen as a position. Instead of talking about personalities, we can talk about "taking positions". This allows people to take many positions and to get interested in other people's positions. In conversations like that it seems easier to take new positions, which gives people the freedom to create changes and to get into developing and challenging conversations about relations between the positions. In difficult conversations (i.e. about something that has to be changed), it seems to be a lot easier to allow changes in a conversation about relations, whereas a conversation about "personality" and how a person needs to change seems to call for feelings of guilt and shame and anger.

When we begin to understand the meaning of "positions", we seem to understand what the other person is saying, and to do things in different ways. We see and listen to the person as if it is "just" a position, and we try to explore why the person takes that particular position. And we can get into conversations about which positions we give each other and how they are alike or different from how we think of ourselves. Here the conversations about understanding each other begin, and our ability to make changes grows. In organizations the managers and staff can begin to think of disagreements between two people as "just two different positions". And that allows the two persons to get interested in each other's thinking. In other words: they get interested in the position the other person takes and why. This is the simplest definition of "dialogue".

Two other statements seem to provide a framework for talking about positions instead of "roles":

"Roles are to be thought of and seen as positions."

"In that way we must see the different roles—that is, chairperson, meeting participants, managers, staff, consultant, children, parents—as positions from which each person can speak and change."

When we talk about a person's role in an organization or in a meeting, we seem to talk about all the things that "complete" the image we have of this person. In many of my consultations I have seen how much time people can spend on talking about a person as if he or she was a concrete and non-changing person, and as if the role *is* this person. The semantic polarity conversation, you might say, invites people to have a conversation where they get interested in "how we see each other and why we say the things that we say". Simply said: people get interested in their relations. In this kind of conversation we invite each other to take a position in the conversation and thereby create a conversation in the best sense of the word.

This statement seems to provide a framework for respecting the positions taken and given:

"When a position is taken or given, it is occupied, and other positions are defined from there."

If a person, A, says to another person, B, *"You are always speaking. I never get to say one word in this meeting"*, it seems to get the conversation stuck in several ways:

1. B has given A the "speaking-position"

2. B has taken the "not-speaking-position"

3. A has taken the "speaking-position"

4. A has given B the "not-speaking-position"

In an ordinary discussion A and B will argue about who is right and who is wrong. It will be a "tug of war", both of them trying to convince the other one, neither of them listening to (or being influenced by) what the other person is saying:

In semantic polarities we say that all you are saying or doing is to be seen as a position. We try to get people to take a position and in open conversations to get interested in what the other person is saying or doing when "taking a position". We talk about how these "taken and given positions" influence each other:

So the questions to use in order to create an open conversation could be:

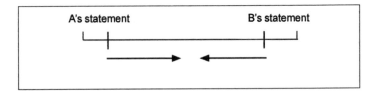

1. A, which position are you taking? And why?
2. B, which position are you taking? And why?
3. A and B, how do your positions relate to each other?
4. What could be interesting for you to talk about now?
5. How will this conversation influence you to change in the future when being in the same meeting?

Sometimes it is easier to understand a theory or ideas through stories about how people have actually been behaving according to the ideas. In my work as a consultant I get a lot of good stories, and here are some examples about taking positions:

a.   A manager in a small firm said in a consultation that he was tired of being the most responsible person in the firm. I drew a polarity line with "taking very much responsibility" at one end and "taking little responsibility" at the other end. The manager took his position at the very end, "taking very much responsibility", and the staff took positions all over the rest of the polarity line. The manager said that the picture said it all: he was the one taking most responsibility. I said that if he wanted things to change he would have to (1) let go of his "position of being the most responsible person in the firm", and (2) notice when his staff surprised him by taking positions that disturbed his picture of them. Then I asked the staff which new positions they wanted to take. And that conversation surprised the manager. They were ready to take a lot more responsibility. From then on, they got into the habit of seeing each other in positions and of talking about their positions. They realized that they could take different positions when they felt the need for it—and they got into a lot of good (and necessary) conversations that made it a lot easier for them to keep creating a better organization. You might say that they went from "post-action", reacting to what had already happened, to "pre-action", feeling on top of the situation.

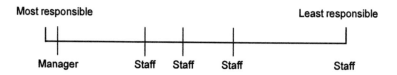

b.   In a private company the manager was seen and understood, also by himself, as not being very caring and compassionate. One of the assistant managers was always seen as the most caring and compassionate person in their department. In a consultation we were working with the whole department, and it became clear that in several ways they were stuck in their conversations because they looked upon each other as being in fixed roles, and that they understood each other's statements and actions according to this perception. We talked about it, and as I introduced the thinking of semantic polarities and positions, I chose to use their fixed idea of "care" and "compassion" in the department. I drew a polarity line:

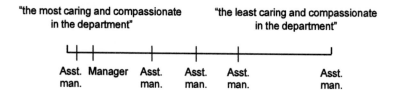

I asked the group to take their positions, and they were surprised that the manager took a position very close to "the most caring and compassionate in the department". Talking about what was behind their positions, the manager said that he had been talking with me when we planned the meeting, and in that conversation he had come to consider that he was very caring and compassionate in the way that he was doing the job of ensuring that the department reached the goal they had to reach in order to keep their jobs. He was aware that the others did not use these words in the same way, and that they were surprised that he saw himself in this way. They got into a new and surprising conversation where they listened to each other, and afterwards we talked about how they could use this kind of conversation in the future.

My purpose was to create a new way for them to be in a conversation. I was not interested in one of them being the most caring and compassionate person in the department, but I was interested in them taking and giving new positions, getting interested in their own and the others' positions, and getting into conversations about their different positions. It worked!

A short presentation of the Growth Model

The Growth Model (Grønbæk & Pors, 2008) is based on the thoughts of semantic polarities and positions (Campbell & Grønbæk, 2006). To avoid any misunderstandings: this model has nothing to do with the GROW model used in coaching in the United Kingdom—I am sorry to say that I do not know anything about that model!

Four years ago I developed the Growth Model at a school that wanted a model for very difficult conversations with parents. The school was using appreciative inquiry (Hammond, 1996), and they could see how children, parents, and teachers were growing by using this approach. They now wanted a conversation model that was respectful towards appreciative inquiry and, on the other hand, would make them able to handle the most difficult situations and conversations. At the same time, they wanted it to be so easy and simple that they could use the model in many other ways and situations. I based the Growth Model on the ideas I believe in: systemic thinking, semantic polarities and positions thinking, and appreciative inquiry. I began developing the Growth Model by basing it on the systemic idea that when we talk about a problem we also assume there is a solution. And then went on from there.

"Problem"   "Solution"

Normally we start with the problem and then find a solution that will match it. In that process, there may be a lot of important conversations that we miss. In the process of developing the Growth Model, it became clear how important these missed conversations are. It also became very clear how important it is to start these conversations with a conversation about all that is going well and that people are doing well—appreciation. It gives a good base to get into the more challenging areas without getting stuck in the language of defence and guilt.

Going well

After talking about all that is going well, we have to talk about the problems, as they are often the reason why we meet and why we need to have these conversations.

"Going well"   "Problems"

In problem-conversations, people seem to get much influenced by the way the conversation gets stuck either because we are very good at talking about finding solutions to the problem or because the "problem-language" is calling for defence and aggression. Anyway, I felt a need for inventing another word for "problems". I decided on: "challenges". And that was an inspiration! Because by talking about "challenges", we were taking the first step towards possibilities. So when we talk about the problem referring to the future, it becomes "a challenge". For example, the problem may be: "only a few people are talking at our meetings". The challenges relating to the problem can be: "it is a challenge to get everybody to talk at the meetings, to get everybody to take a clear position in our discussions, to get those who talk to listen more, to get more statements out in the open."

"Going well"   "Challenges"

In the language of the semantic polarities model, we now have the two opposite statements–positions. But the semantic polarities model goes beyond that. The whole idea of semantic polarities is to see and get interested in understanding what lies behind the two positions. And in that conversation where both positions are being carefully heard, we create the dialogue between the two positions. The connection between the two positions is "possibilities":

"Going well"   "Challenges"

_____

Possibilities

We want everybody in the meeting or conversation to take a position that is clear and is spoken out loudly to everybody in the conversation: which possibility or possibilities do you see that can help in fulfilling the challenges?

Most meetings or conversations stop here, but the Growth Model goes beyond that. The conversation continues by everybody taking positions about the "possibilities". We call it making agreements. All persons commit themselves to act on at least one of the possibilities; two or more persons can choose the same possibility. In this way, a whole set of efficient changes will be initiated.

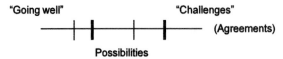

Possibilities

The Growth Model invites all participants in a meeting to join the conversation and to take a clear and strong position in agreements and obligations. The Growth Model has proved its efficiency in many different situations. We use it in schools for meetings with parents and children, as well as in consultations with organizations in order to create development in a certain situation, for staff and managers, or in the organization as a whole. It has been used in many different conversations with great success—often as a supplement to semantic polarities. We find that the Growth Model offers a framework for a conversation in which people take very clear positions and commit themselves to actions that will make the changes they have been talking about come true.

The Growth Model — visualized

We visualize the model using circles. All statements are written around a circle:

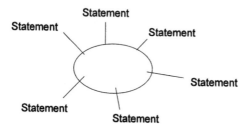

In this way there is priority connected to all the statements. They are all equal. The Growth Model consists of five such circles (Figure 5.1). The five circles form the agenda for the meeting or the conversation.

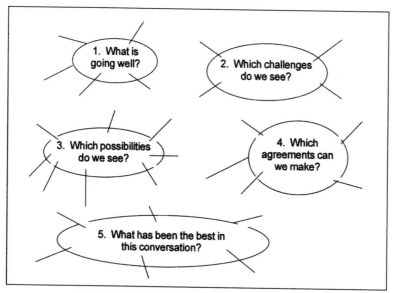

Figure 5.1.   The Growth Model

Outline of the case study

The following case is from my work as a consultant. I hope it will simplify the thoughts and the ideas described above. Along with telling the story, I give my reflections about my work as a systemic consultant. Feel free to agree or disagree with the reflections—that is, just to take a position on "changes" and on "developments of your own thinking".

I have chosen a case that will lead you through a consultation that I did in a school where the managers wanted the staff to handle their meetings and decision-making in a much better way than they used to do. The managers called me because they did not believe in just telling people what to do, but wanted the consultation to be a process where people could take positions in the conversations and the changes. The managers believed that the process would create much better and more relevant changes because every member of the staff, the management, and the School Board would be present.

I agreed with the managers on the programme for the day. In the following description, I follow the "programme" for the consultation.

The case

I was called in by the headmaster and the deputy of an independent school. They wanted to change the culture of their meetings and of the way they made decisions in all of the different departments of the school. They had called me because they knew me from workshops and because they liked the ideas and the models I was using. They wanted the members of the School Board and the whole staff of managers, teachers, secretaries, cleaners, and helpers to have the experience of being in the same process of development together. They had very high expectations for the day we had planned.

The school (350 children, aged 6 to 17 years) had asked me to help them develop their work environment in relation to their meetings and their decision-making. I was to work with 50 people: managers, teachers, secretaries, caretakers, and Board members. For some time the school had been focusing on the psychological work environment. The day meeting was supposed to provide everyone with a kick in the direction of becoming a better school and with ways in which everybody in the staff and on the Board could contribute to this objective. It was important for the managers that all the staff and Board members would take part in the conversations and take responsibility for creating a better meeting and decision-making culture.

The group of managers (the Principal and two managers) and I had a meeting where we decided on the focus for the day—*their meeting and decision-making culture*—and the process was to focus on the importance of the entire group taking part in the process of change. Each person was to feel and see the possibilities of changes, and they had to be involved in taking the decision about the changes and the new ways of having meetings and making decisions.

The managers thought that it would be a good idea to give the staff a set of rules to be used in their meetings. The rules could be: "Everybody must listen", "Everybody must speak his or her mind", "Everybody must respect the chairperson". In this way, as managers, they would not have to point out the importance of "listening", "speaking up", "respecting the chairperson", and so on. The managers really wanted the staff to take responsibility in the meetings and for decisions, and they were convinced that I had "a set of rules" to be used in meetings and decision-making. The managers identified several "problems" in their meetings: "*big differences in the cultures*", "*authority levels*", "*we are all equal—no feeling of chairperson's authority*", "*the others are responsible*", "*the need for rules and strategies concerning meetings and decision-making processes*". I said that instead of giving them "new rules" I thought it would be better if each person reflected on his/her own part and possibilities of making the best meetings. The managers agreed on that. To make a more clear understanding between us I made a semantic polarity:

"Rules and tools will create the best meetings and decisions"	"Being aware of your own and others' positions will create the best meetings and decisions"

"Creating good meetings and decisions"

I explained that it would allow all the staff and the board members to take positions and to speak from their positions. In that way we would create a conversation that would allow differences. In order to get them to use the conversations in their meetings, I would introduce the background and the ideas behind semantic polarities and positioning, including some thoughts on appreciative inquiry. I would use the Growth Model in practice and then talk about the theory afterwards. The managers liked this way of thinking better than the idea of giving rules. We agreed on using their wonderful, newly built, circular music hall for the session. We chose this special room for a special meeting. Right from the start, we wanted to give everybody a feeling of a meeting that was different from what they were used to.

My reflections

In my many years of consulting I have found it easy, yet very efficient, to create the space for personal changes by using the ideas of semantic polarities and positioning. As soon as people get a tool that they understand and are able to use themselves, they take strong personal positions and step into changes in a powerful, easy, respectful, and playful way.

I am very fond of this tool or model because a whole consultation process seems to be one long "journey" of personal and team reflections. People see how easily they can take positions in what they used to think was very difficult conversations about problems or changes. The ease and lightness create hope and joy—and that makes the big difference for the consultant!

I think that people try to avoid changes they cannot imagine, understand, or see. It is easy for consultants to "teach models and tell people what to do". Systemic consultation is, to me, to explore the positions people take and the possibility for people to change positions. One might say that instead of "showing and internalizing a needed change in the organizations" we consultants need to create conversations about the "awareness of taking positions and positioning others in order to keep changing" and "feeling aware of and taking part in the changes".

Working with the ideas of semantic polarities and positioning gives people and organizations a chance to see how simple and easy it is to keep positioning themselves and others, including after the consultant "has left the building". In that way "taking positions and being positioned" is helping people and organizations to be in the process of needed and wanted change over time—again and again.

Back to the story

The managers and I agreed on this plan for the day:

Headlines for the day:

Meeting and decision culture:

How do I influence myself and others?

Which position do I take in the meeting?

How do I position others?

The culture of an organization is constantly created by the people in the organization. In that way we are all co-creators of our culture. In order to take a simple approach to this thinking about "culture", I wrote three statements on the flip chart:

"What we do creates our reality"

"What we say reflects our responsibility"

"When I inspire others, I inspire myself"

These statements were to be used throughout the day in order to stay in the process of "taking positions".

The programme for the day:

1. *Welcome and short presentation (the Principal and MG).*
2. *Warming-up exercise.*
3. *Short presentation of the thoughts behind semantic polarities.*
4. *From problems to polarity lines: exercises related to positioning.*
5. *Short presentation of the Growth Model and how it can be used in meetings.*
6. *A conversation about what has been learned during the whole day.*
7. *Conclusions and thanks for the day we have all spent together.*

Session 1.   Welcome and short presentation

The Principal introduced me both on a personal level and as a consultant. He expressed his great expectations of my ability to teach them something helpful as well as to work with them through a good process. He said that they had attended one of my seminars, and it had been one of the most instructive and inspiring experiences they had had.

My reflections

If a word or a subject is mentioned, we also "hear" the opposite word or the "not do" and "not good". In conversations as a consultant I am aware of the fact that if a person feels that it is very important to tell a good story, there have been bad stories as well. I am also aware of the fact that if a bad story is being told, the person has the idea that there may be a good story somewhere. From the introduction the Principal made, you might say that I was positioned on a polarity line with "doing very well" at one end and "doing not so well" at the other end. I chose to take a position very close to "doing very well".

In order to get started as quickly as possible, I often start with an exercise inspired by appreciative inquiry, where we focus on and talk about all the good stories about others and ourselves. The purpose is to get people into a good relationship with a pleasant feeling and some laughter. It is my experience that when people get to tell a good story and to listen to other people's good stories, they smile and laugh. And if I, the consultant, want people to get into a process of change and respond to other people's changes, I have to do it the "easiest" way. So I chose an exercise that was one of my "easiest" in order to get a good start.

Back to the story

Session 2.   Warming-up exercise

I asked the group to walk around and find three other people with whom they did not talk in their daily work and with whom they would like to talk. Then I gave them the exercise:

a. *Think about a good story from your work with each other or with the children.*

b. *Stand in groups of four, tell your story, and listen to the other stories for 15 minutes. The stories are not to be commented on by the others in the group.*

After 15 minutes I called the whole group together, and we talked in plenary about what they had felt was nice about the exercise. They were amazed that they could talk so easily with people they hardly knew. They had a good time. They had laughed. They had found it hard to tell good stories about themselves. It had been easier to listen to the stories of the others. They did not get around to listening to all the stories, because there was too little time.

I said that we would do the exercise again in new groups, and this time they should keep track of the time.

After the second round, we talked about how they managed to get all the stories told and heard. They said that they listened in a better way—more intensely and focused upon the person and less on their own thoughts and reflections. They said that they had kept the rule I gave them about not commenting on the stories.

We talked about how they could use this experience in their meetings. They laughed, and I was being positioned in the "doing very well" position.

My reflections

By telling these stories and by drawing some polarity lines I had tried to "show the picture". The group got interested in the "lines" and the thoughts behind them. Now I wanted them to play with the "lines" and get into conversations about their meetings and decision-making. In a way you can say that I wanted to use the semantic polarity conversation model in order to get them to talk about their "problems in meetings and making decisions" in a new and inspiring way in order to get them to talk and to listen to each other in and from "new positions".

Back to the story

Session 3.   Short presentation of the thoughts
              behind semantic polarities

The presentation I did is the same as in the description at the beginning of this chapter.

Session 4.   From problems to polarity lines:
              exercises related to positioning

The managers had given me some thoughts about the difficulties in their meetings and their discussions. I had changed these difficulties into four semantic polarity lines. The whole group was to work in smaller groups with the same polarity line simultaneously—one at a time.

I said that I had created the four semantic polarity lines about "meetings" from the talk I had with the managers. After each of the semantic polarities, we would talk about what they had just learned about their meetings.

Five flip charts had been placed around the room. I asked the group to get together in five equally sized groups—beginning by getting together in groups with people they knew the least. They were to use the flip charts, standing or sitting around the flip chart so that everybody in their group could see it and write on it.

I instructed the whole group:

» how to draw the first polarity line on their flip chart
» to "take their own position" by taking the pen and drawing their own positions on the polarity lines
» for each to take their position without comments and then get into a conversation about what was behind each position.

I underlined the fact that is was the conversation "around" and behind the positions that was important.

They worked with each polarity line for 20 minutes. Then we had a quick plenary with comments and talked about what they had learned, and then they shifted to new groups standing around a flip chart for the next semantic polarity line.

The four polarity lines about "meetings" were:

"I am best at talking"	"I am best at listening"
―――――――――――――	―――――――――――――

"I find the process most important"	"I find the decisions most important"
―――――――――――――	―――――――――――――

"I think it is most important to stop talking when the meeting time is over"	"I think it is most important to prolong the meeting and continue talking"
―――――――――――――	―――――――――――――

"The chairperson is responsible"	"All participants in the meeting are responsible"
―――――――――――――	―――――――――――――

After the last round of taking positions and talking about them, we had a joint conversation about what they had just learned about their meetings and decision-making. They said—and I wrote it on a flip chart—that they had found out how important it was for them

» to listen to each other
» to talk in the same direction (about the same issue at the same time)
» to let people finish what they wanted to say
» to participate in the conversation with "their positions"
» to have this model in mind when they were talking—not only in meetings, but also when just talking with each other.

We agreed that these five items were to be hung up in their meeting room so that they could glance at it if needed and would allow each other to refer to the items in order to get into conversations like the one they had just had.

My reflections

To all this you might say: So what! These items are well known—common knowledge! Yes! This is common knowledge, but if we all always did what we know we should do, there would be no need for systemic consultations. The thing is that we do know what to do, but we need to talk about what we do and talk ourselves into doing it. I think we have to be in constructive conversations and to talk and listen in order to explore and then change our habits through our conversations. It is also well known that people seem to be able to implement their own (brilliant) ideas rather than doing what other people want them to do. We have different conversations in order to create the thoughts, make the changes, and for these to be seen as the (new) habit.

Especially as a consultant, and as a guest in the organization, I find it very necessary that people talk themselves into the knowledge and the changes they want to create. That is, for me, the easiest way for a consultant to create changes that will last for a longer period than until the moment the consultant has "left the building". It also visualizes a path they can choose to take in order to make more successful changes. In this way, the consultant can come back and be part of a new development and new changes instead of repairing and repeating her/himself. And to me this is a way of being "alive" as a consultant, reproducing my own energy and commitment. It makes me feel proud, and it makes me feel the joy of being a consultant.

Being a consultant well known for developing new models and concepts for organizations, I was asked in 2004 by a school to create a concept for conversations. The conversations were to be:

- » based on appreciation of all participants in a conversation
- » dealing with "the problem"
- » accepting the differences between being a teacher, a parent, or a child
- » making agreed promises very clear
- » ensuring that everybody would keep the promises made
- » used in many different situations and conversations
- » so easy and simple that everybody (teacher, pedagogue, parent, and child) could understand and use them.

That could be thought about as "not possible" at one end of a polarity line and "possible" at the other end. I chose the position at the "possible" end. So I said: That seems like a "piece of cake"! And, I thought, it was just a matter of putting together "appreciation and semantic polarities and positions" in a simple model.

The Growth Model has now been presented to and used by many people in different organizations. It has been developed as a conversation model for different conversations between people at equal levels, between school and parents, in management, in job interviews, and in developing organizations (Grønbæk & Pors, 2008; Grønbæk, Pors, Campbell, & Pors, 2008).

Back to the story

Session 5.   Short presentation of the Growth Model
             and how it can be used in meetings

In order to take the next step with the group, I chose to tell the story behind the Growth Model and then talk and visualize the way through the model. I often describe the background for the model in order to get people to take a position in the idea and then to use and to develop the model. I presented the model (the same presentation as above), and afterwards I asked the whole group to get together in their "natural groups", teachers, secretaries, managers, Board members. In these groups they were to use the Growth Model to talk about the Growth Model and semantic polarities:

1. In which way could it be helpful for them to use the Growth Model and semantic polarities?
2. Which challenges did they see?
3. Which possibilities did they see in relation to the challenges?
4. Which agreements were they ready to commit themselves to?
5. What had been the best part of this exercise?

This was just an exercise to get them to work with the model in practice. In my previous meeting with the managers, we had agreed on these models being presented in order to be used in their future meetings.

My reflections

Using semantic polarities and positions and the Growth Model is easy for me because it gives me the energy and the joy that are needed in consultations. If a consultant positions her/himself as "this is an impossible case", it will influence the consultation. In order to see the possibilities and to have the energy to guide, present, and cope with whatever is being brought up, it is important for me to have effective tools that I can work with and that work for me. Semantic polarities and the Growth Model are some of my most used tools. I often use them in different combinations. I will leave it to you as readers to create some combinations that will work for you.

Back to the story

Session 6.   A conversation about what has been learned during the whole day

We were now getting to the end of the day. It was important for me to help the group and the organization to become more aware of what we had been doing, and what they had learned that they wanted to use in their meetings and in their decision-making after this day. Also I wanted them to reflect on how to use the models elsewhere in their daily work.

I asked the whole group to talk in the same "natural" groups about their meetings. They were to use the flip charts to draw the five circles (the Growth Model), one circle at a time, and each person was to write his or her own statements on it.

In the following plenary we looked at all their circles, and then I asked them in the same groups to talk about what new thoughts about their meetings they had developed during the whole day, and what they wanted to do from now on in order to create the best meetings.

They said that they wanted to use the models, and the "rules" in the models, during their meetings and decision-making. The rules should make them focus on the importance of talking and listening from and in positions. We laughed, and I told them that we, the managers and I, had talked about rules and had chosen not to make up rules for them—and now they had made the rules themselves. They said that the process had given them the space to create the rules, and that they could respect them because they, themselves, had been involved in the process. I said that they had taken positions in their difficulties and in developing new ideas and had then taken new positions in the new ideas.

We then talked about how they could use the same process in the classroom.

My reflections

The story is about the consultant creating the space for safe and stimulating conversations that will have an impact for more than one week after the consultation. In this process, I find it very helpful to let people talk themselves into their own implementation. This may seem to be a very ordinary statement to many consultants. But I have been working with many organizations where they had worked with many changes and had not been able to see how the changes had made an impact on the organization or the people in the organization. Changes and implementations that will make a difference must be an internal process that the consultant must be aware of in order to create the right atmosphere for a process and a dialogue that will turn the changes into a new daily practice that will be seen and felt as good and constructive for the working relationships.

Back to the story

Session 7.   Conclusions and thanks
              for the day we have all spent together

Working with an agenda given by the managers for the day, I think it is important to hand the agenda back to the managers and the organization. During the day the managers had allowed the staff and the Board members to be in conversations together and with a consultant to navigate when reflections from the managers would come in useful. During the whole day the managers had been positioned as positive observers. It is very important that observers give their observations back to the group they have been observing. So I had instructed the managers to give their observations back to the group in a positive way during the day. If they were to say something "negative", they had to express it as a "challenge".

After each exercise the managers spoke together about which positive things they had seen and heard, and what had surprised them positively. They did that very well and very positively. In that way they stressed very clearly in which direction they wanted the organization to grow, and how they would support and facilitate this process. Thus, the managers took a clear position in the process without taking the lead.

Now was the time for the consultant to give back the agenda to the managers and to the organization.

I started this closing-up conversation by thanking the managers for giving me the opportunity to create this day with them. I said that I thought that the managers

» gave the discourse for the day and the changes by hiring me
» showed the way by taking clear positions in what was going on
» demonstrated a culture of listening when decisions were being made in order to create the best organization
» showed that they had learned new ways of talking about difficult matters in a very constructive way and in a way of taking action during the session

I then addressed the group and said that I had been very impressed by their energy and their way of taking new ideas so easily into their own way of thinking. I thanked them for being good listeners to each other and for the way they—already during the session—had taken in the new positions they had talked about. So they had already made some of the changes they had said that they wanted to make.

Then I asked each of the managers to talk about what had

made them really happy, really proud, and really anxious during the day. And the staff and the Board members took very strong listening positions and said they were happy to hear what the managers said.

They said they had had a very interesting day, with a lot of hope for their future. They were happy about the tools, and they felt that they would be able to use the tools first thing Monday morning. They thought that not only had they got new models, they had also felt they had created them themselves along the way, and by using them they already felt acquainted with them.

We agreed they should work with the models and send their reflections to me, and they said they would be proud to do so.

The feedback to the consultant was that everybody was enthusiastic and energetic about all their thoughts and all the exercises. We agreed on a follow-up in the New Year.

A small curio:

When the managers and I first agreed on the day, we decided on 8 hours for the process. For different reasons we had to cut it down to only 5½ hours. The managers wanted to maintain the same programme, which I accepted, provided that we were not having long breaks. But how should we explain that to the staff and Board members, who had all been at work from 8 a.m. till 1 p.m. and then were expected to be engaged and active in our session from 1.30 to 6.30 without breaks?

I said it was the managers who had to tell the participants about this "little" agreement. And they did—in a very clear and positive way. I thought I had to address the issue as well. So I started the session by drawing a scale on the flip chart:

I explained that we had shortened the session by 2½ hours, but that they did not have to worry because the 2½ hours were the breaks, so we would be able to do all that they had wanted to do in the course of 5½ hours. They all laughed, and I promised them that they were going to be included in a very active way in the whole process. And they were! I was very impressed with their engagement in their school, in each other, and in the models that I had told them about.

Critique of the models used

A manager was applying for a new job. At the interview he was asked about his strengths and weaknesses. He told about his strengths for a long time and when he was to tell about his weaknesses he said that he could not think about any. They all smiled and asked why. He said that in his current job he did not use his weaknesses, so he did not think about them because in his daily work he focused on all the things that worked well in the job and on the successes of his employees. They all smiled again, and then they asked if they could talk to his deputy. He gave his permission. The next day his deputy came to him, smiled, and said that someone called her and asked her questions about him and his weaknesses as a manager. She said that she had told them that she could not think of any. They both laughed and talked about how they had succeeded in having a positive focus in the organization. Not that they didn't make mistakes or had weaknesses, but that they did not pay any attention to them.

When he told his wife the story, she said: *Oh, they should have talked with me!!*

This little anecdote was just to underline the fact that I generally tend to focus on the strengths rather than the limitations. You can put the two thoughts—"focusing on strengths" and "focusing on limitations"—at either end of a polarity line. And on that line I would take a position close to "focusing on strengths". But the whole idea of putting them on the same polarity line is to create a conversation that connects the two ends. In that way, both thoughts will give meaning to each other. In order to talk about "strengths" you need to talk about "limitations".

Strengths

The two models—semantic polarities and the Growth Model—that I have described here are based on the thoughts of "what works well". I think that the three main strengths are that both models

» create safe and developing conversations, even about difficult matters
» are simple and easy to use in many different situations
» engage people in challenging conversations.

In this way, the models can be developed in order to create the best conversation, the best situation, and the best organization.

Limitations

I think the main limitation is that the focus on the models can disturb the necessary focus on the conversation they create and the people participating in the conversation.

As I said previously: I think that it is very important that "people meet people" (i.e., consultants) and not models or methods.

CHAPTER SIX

Surviving the task of management

Rita Harris

Commentary

Rita Harris's chapter illustrates how she uses systemic thinking and practice in her teaching and consultation to managers in the public sector in the United Kingdom, drawing on her own long experience as a manager in the NHS.

She describes the preoccupations of managers arising from the public sector context in the United Kingdom, with its environment of cross-agency working, collaboration, driving towards targets and performance, and the constant need to change while engaging all staff in the process.

A theme that comes through clearly in the case examples is the splits that can develop between managers and clinicians and the attempt that is made by clinicians to isolate and disconnect from the management task because this appears to be connected to the limitation of resources that clinicians need to do their work. Hence, it seems essential for managers to hone their systemic thinking so they can understand how whole-system dynamics like this can marginalize them and potentially render them ineffective unless they can understand and work with them differently. Harris suggests some good ways managers can engage the whole system in organizational change.

Another interesting theme is the challenges of multi-agency working. One of the paradoxes she describes is that, in order for several agencies to work together well with agreed codes of practice and so on, it is important for the individual agencies involved to have more of a sense of their individual identity rather than less. This appears to be related to the tendency in multi-agency working for staff to want to avoid rivalry or polarity between separate agencies. This can result in a "dumbing down" of the overall debate and a loss of identity both in the whole organization and its constituent parts.   [Eds.]

In this chapter I describe ways in which I have applied systemic ideas in my teaching and consultation to managers in the public sector. I have been a manager within the National Health Service for many years and have had the privilege of working with managers both in health and in education, as a colleague, a teacher/trainer, and a consultant. During the last ten years I have developed, with colleagues, a training programme for clinical and educational psychology managers and more recently for other managers working in children's services. During this process I have acted as both trainer and consultant to a variety of managers, and it is this experience that I shall be drawing upon in this chapter. The course has been described elsewhere (Harris, 2005) and is delivered in two blocks of three days of (intensive) seminars and workshops separated by a gap of six months. Course members develop a systemic framework and understanding of organizations that they can apply to their own work contexts via a mixture of formal teaching and experiential exercises. During the six-month course, members complete a project in which they are required to apply the systemic ideas from the course and their reading to a management task in which they are engaged. This they are required to negotiate with their line manager.

In this chapter I describe some of the issues preoccupying managers I have worked with and outline ways we have worked together to help them understand and work within the systems of which they are a part.

Throughout the process of working with managers, I have taken from systemic and social constructionist theory ideas that have been particularly helpful in working as a consultant to managers. Although the content and preoccupations of managers have changed somewhat over time, the ideas and practice from systemic theory that they have found most helpful have been the same. In essence, the model I have used is one that develops in managers a reflective stance that enables them to become more observant of the processes of which they are a part. The ideas and practice that many have found most helpful in this process include:

» the interconnectedness of systems
» the importance of context in understanding the meaning of actions and relationships and how organizational culture develops
» the beliefs or assumptions underlying these
» how voices do or do not get heard
» the fit between individual needs and those of the organization (Harris, 2005).

Preoccupations of managers

Systemic thinking has been particularly helpful for managers in a context of national/major change to professional services in the public sector brought about by new legislation. Many of the managers I have worked with have been in children's services, for which the greater integration of agencies has often raised fundamental questions about management and accountability, such as a greater separation of operational and professional management. Systemic thinking allows styles of management to emerge that attempt to address some of the real tensions current in multi-agency/multi-professional work. As services develop and change, so we are challenged to think in different ways about the task of management. As managers become more actively involved at commissioning levels, the dangers of looking upwards and outwards and losing touch with grassroots staff can become apparent.

Marketplace strategies that encourage survival of the fittest with financial stringencies can hit core professional identities hard. For the value-based organizations of the public sector that do not fit a business model, the challenge for managers is how to manage and lead organizations that will survive but maintain the core values and identities within new contexts that are also able to deliver effective patient/user care and services. In my experience, a style of management that focuses on low levels of control and high levels of professional autonomy, which assumes that aspects of accountability are shared across teams, is necessary but challenging. This style of management requires, in my view, leadership skill in order to deliver effective services but within a clear framework for service delivery.

Many of the issues course participants have faced fall into the following clusters:

» organizations moving towards integrated professional structures and across agency collaboration, which raise issues of cross-organizational culture work
» issues of professional identity and challenges to professional value systems
» leadership skills versus those of management
» styles of management and leadership—autonomy versus control
» concerns about capacity to reflect on service development, delivery, and good practice
» managing the pace of change and commitment to new learning
» finding ways of engaging in the process of change.

Key ideas in working with managers

Observing systems

In order to generate and attend to feedback, to understand the systems of which they are a part, managers found the idea of taking an observer position extremely helpful. This is no easy task, and developing ways of maintaining a neutral stance characterized by curiosity has been helpful in enabling managers to ask questions that generate and allow them to attend to feedback about the core beliefs and values held by individuals and organizations. The focus has often been on exploring the potential losses and gains in organizational change and on identifying some of the tensions and dilemmas that emerge. Mapping the key stakeholders within any system has been a helpful starting point for many of the managers with whom I have worked, and using hypothesizing and circular questioning as means of identifying multiple realities and allowing marginalized discourses/narratives to emerge has been extremely helpful. An exercise designed to facilitate this process is presented in Exhibit 6.1. One participant, appointed to promote social inclusion within a local education authority (LEA), was struggling to implement a policy that he had been mandated by his service to lead on. By stepping back from the task and "mapping the system", he moved to a position of understanding his task to be establishing a role and mandate beyond his immediate professional grouping within the LEA. Having widened the task, he then sought feedback from other key players about their understanding of social inclusion, their roles within this, how they

---

EXHIBIT 6.1
Pair exercise 1—Mapping the system

1. What is the vision/service rationale?
2. Who are the key players?
3. What are the points of emphasis in the service?
4. What are the problems/dilemmas faced?
5. Who else is involved or affected?
6. What are the lines of accountability?
7. How do views get sanction/authority?
8. What are the strengths of the organization?
9. What are the choices/options available?
10. What are the constraints/environmental limitations?

understood his role, and the interrelatedness of each service. From this a borough-wide plan was developed, with opportunities for feedback and review built in.

Feedback

A system needs feedback to know itself, and in times of change, conflict, and difficulty pools of information and feedback often dry up. Staff can become suspicious and anxious, misinformation abounds, and gaps in communication can be filled by fears and fantasies. Greater transparency, together with exploration and discussion of anxieties and dilemmas, is something that all managers found difficult to contemplate but often the most helpful. One newly appointed manager found herself and her service not part of and disconnected from a central data-collection exercise of which they felt they had no ownership and was of no relevance to their service. Staff had refused to collect the data required for this reason. However, by placing the team outside the system, they were restricting information flow from the service to more senior managers and thereby excluding the service from any meaningful feedback from them. This particular manager found the metaphor of the manager patrolling the perimeters of the system and negotiating input and output very helpful at this stage. She responded by inviting to a team meeting the person whose task it was to collect the data and analyse it. There they discovered that the person whose task it was to collect information about their service and report on it to their commissioners did not understand what they had been set up to do. They also discovered that this information officer also felt isolated and disconnected from her task. The team therefore worked together with this officer to develop a data set relevant to their task. The officer, in turn, fed back her excitement at working constructively with one of the teams within the trust. This manager responded by placing the team in better contact and communication with the external parts of the system to enable an efficient feedback loop and for the development to be creative rather than defended against. She also engaged the team in exploring the match or fit between how they felt others perceived and saw the service and what they themselves were striving to do and present to others. This enabled an exploration of the beliefs and fears about those outside the service who were evaluating it.

One consequence of this exploration was that individual roles and differences within the team also emerged, in addition to those in the relationship between the team and the external environment. In the view of this particular manager, her role in negotiating individual and service needs is a constant challenge. For her, by hypothesizing about the situation she found herself in and generating questions to explore this, she was able to facilitate both the team to think about itself and a personal reflection for herself in her role as manager.

In the public sector, the drive for outcome-focused objectives can make it easy for managers to underestimate the complexity of the organizational processes required to achieve them. This can lead to frustration and disillusionment in staff as well as a huge waste of effort and commitment. The amount of time spent in developing new formats for data management can be largely wasted when seen as disconnected from the main task of the staff involved. The result can be incomplete or, at worst, erroneous data. This particularly arises when those required to undertake the work can see that the key factors have been omitted from management planning, driven as it frequently is by externally imposed time scales or mismatched priorities. Aspects of systemic thinking, such as the underlying beliefs and value systems that individuals bring to their work and how these fit with the organizational task, can enable people to take account of the complexity of organizational service-delivery environments and of how managers and staff understand and react to these.

An example of applying systemic thinking to developing a new role

Another manager, working in an artificial-limb service providing prosthetic limbs for people who have had an amputation, was the only mental health professional in a multidisciplinary team dedicated to post-amputation care. During the course we worked in small reflecting teams (Andersen, 1987), with an interviewer, interviewee, and one or two observers. In these exercises the interviewer uses systemic questions, and discussions between the interviewer and the observers are held openly in front of the interviewee. This process enables the interviewee to hear and internalize a different conversation, rather than just different explanations, and therefore provides an opportunity for reflection. This manager was struck by the reactions of the other clinicians to his role, as something separate and disconnected from the ongoing work of the unit, and was able to reflect on these as a way of understanding the challenge faced by the organization. For example, if emotions from service users arose, it was easier to ignore them, channel them into technical issues, or simply refer on. He reflected on the emotions and reactions that he was experiencing, and at times on his own responses, as a signal of the organizational reality, which he was able to use to glean information about the organization. Viewing his experience through this lens, he began to hypothesize that, rather than the mental health professional being separate, psychological aspects of the work were being distanced by the organization. His hypothesis was that the reactions to his arrival were a reflection of the way the organization dealt with the emotional issues associated with illness and disability—they distanced emotional aspects and focused on the technical aspects. This resonates with the earlier work of Menzies Lyth (Menzies, 1959) and has been developed further (Armstrong, 2004).

For this manager the shift from individual pathology models towards a systemic approach, in which he began to understand the responses of others to his role as linked to individual and organizational beliefs and anxieties, provided valuable information about how to manage the organizational change inherent in the appointment of a mental health professional. He began to look differently at the behaviour and stories he was experiencing—for example, he saw the arrival of a mental health professional as a change in and a challenge to the system and to the accepted, or privileged, ways of thinking and behaving. He understood the reactions to him, and at times his own reactions, as ways of understanding the organizational reality. His response to this feedback was to set up a way of working that was opposite to that which might have been expected. Rather than being separate, he began to work very closely with the multidisciplinary team.

Regular consultancy is not such a common characteristic of physical health settings as it might be in mental health settings. However, this manager encouraged consultancy at both an individual-case and organizational level within his role. One situation he faced was in being given the task of deciding whether a particular form of treatment, linked to body image following major surgery, should be given to patients. Rather than take up this "gate-keeping" role, he was encouraged to explore the situation more fully. First he mapped the network of professionals involved, in discussion at all levels of the organization. Then he explored with individual clinicians and managers their thoughts, feelings, and ideas about the issue and how this was influenced by their professional and personal experiences. This manager found his lack of technical knowledge helpful in remaining curious, and he used circular questioning to make links between individuals' beliefs and behaviour, particularly in relation to what were difficult and emotive decisions. He asked what individuals thought about this particular treatment, in terms of the effect on patients and how this in turn affected the way they felt and behaved. He encouraged staff to tell their stories of what brought them into this work and the experiences that shaped their current views. In meetings he asked staff to reflect on the impact of what others thought and said on their own ideas. As the key ideas and dilemmas emerged, including a strongly held assumption that all patients would want this scarce and particular form of treatment, the staff group agreed that body image was an important issue for them all to consider and that they should work together to understand the needs of each patient in this respect. Indeed, as the team developed a more psychological approach to their treatment decisions and were able to respond to individual needs, they discovered that not everyone wanted the treatment they had expected and had been fearful of not being able to provide. This example raises the issue of how teams will tend to avoid facing what they perceive to be difficult decisions by giving this to one member of the team, who may take this on in his or her "expert role", at the expense of responding to the needs of individual patients.

Introducing unexpected ideas

Many of the managers I have worked with have commented on how organizational change has occurred in incremental and often surprising ways. One participant on the course found the idea of introducing very small but surprising ideas very helpful. She identified the importance of carefully listening to the value systems of all those concerned and building on feedback to widen the perspective of the staff group and to introduce new and creative ideas. As a principal educational psychologist heading up an educational psychology and learning support service, she created separate teams of advisory teachers in order to enhance joint working with their educational psychology colleagues. All those in her service were committed to joint working, and this had always been led by the educational psychologists (EPs) and was not experienced as working well. As she explored the views and values of the teaching staff, they were able to make explicit their discontent with the perceived differences in the way their and the EPs' roles were valued and with the real differences in terms of pay. Rather than accept what was apparently a positive move—that is, towards more integrated working—she slowly and carefully unpicked the values and beliefs that each group held about their work and roles and the perceived value of these. What emerged was an implicit tension between joint working and a sense that, by doing so, the value of the support teachers was being lost. Her intervention was to redress this balance in order to facilitate the two groups working together. The idea of increased separateness in order to facilitate better joint working was seen as surprising but effective. This links to the question of fit, which I explore in more detail below (see also Campbell, Coldicott, & Kinsella, 1994; Cecchin, 1987).

Leadership and multi-agency work

Most recently managers have been commenting on how the demands of external factors/drivers have at times distanced them from their internal organization. When gathering feedback from the most recent cohort of those attending the management training course, this seemed to be linked in part to the increased emphasis on multi-agency working. When exploring the option of broadening this course to managers of children's services across agencies, we were met with the anxiety that "multi-agency means no one's needs are met". When explored in more detail this seemed to reflect a very real concern that a focus on multi-agency working was eroding professional identity and skill base. Paradoxically it is commonly understood/felt that having a clear sense of professional identity and worth is part of what facilitates effective multidisciplinary and multi-agency work. Within the public sector, much time and thought has gone into how members of different professions can work together most effectively to meet the needs of populations they serve. The focus on multi-agency work not only requires those with different professional backgrounds to work together effectively, but also brings together different cultures such as health and social care. Each of these has their own core beliefs about effective outcomes, ways of measuring and monitoring these, and organizational structures to deliver them.

While one cannot deny the value of the ideas behind integration of services, particularly for children and young people, many are experiencing this agenda as over-mechanistic and driven by the need for rapid change. This fails to take into account the complex understanding of the roles that public sector staff build up, as a response to the huge diversity and complexity of needs of the people they serve, in developing frameworks to meet these. Most managers I have worked with have recognized the need to invest in this complexity and that the existing structures cannot change too quickly without threatening the intrinsic values that drive that commitment (Booker, 2005). This requires management of core tasks and leadership that allows a proactive and forward-thinking approach.

According to the Centre for Leadership's Review of Leadership Theory (Bolden, Gosling, Marturano, & Dennison, 2003), few leadership frameworks appear to promote the importance of the leader's listening skills and the importance of followers (i.e., that people need to follow the leader or there is no leadership). Listening and working to encourage and help people to follow and develop ideas seemed to be crucial in developing new organizational cultures and building on existing ones. The Learning and Skills Research Centre concludes that leadership theories pay little attention to process and context. A systemic model would suggest that relational models of leadership are most helpful in this arena. There are, of course, some notable exceptions (Armstrong, 2004; McKenna, 2000; Obholzer & Miller, 2004; Obholzer & Roberts, 1994).

Changing contexts

Of particular interest is that over time the changing nature of the feedback to the course and the experience of managers reflect the particular contexts in which they find themselves. In 2006 the feedback was an enhanced sense of limited time to reflect and to find a space for oneself in reflecting on the task of management. While the previous year had focused on marginalized voices and discourses, this current cohort were preoccupied with the notions of leadership and partnership working and the tension that can occur between operational and professional lines of management. This, I am sure, reflects the speed of change and movement towards integrated children's services, and one of the outcomes of this appears to be a challenge to traditional professional identities. The Children Act 2004 requires partnership working across all agencies in a local authority area and the bringing together of education and social care services into local authority children's services. The role of users, particularly taking their views into account, is high on the current government's agenda. The move towards greater integration of children's services may also be understood as a response of public sector organizations attempting to adapt to increased demands for more shared responsibility for outcomes. Behind these agendas is a speed of change that managers experienced as disconnecting the organization from the underlying assumptions and values that led people to work in the public sector. Many experienced an assumption that gradual or phased change was perceived as superficial rather than being a deeper conceptual change (Booker, 2005).

Booker (2005) hypothesizes that for some policymakers there is a belief that gradual change is a way of attempting to achieve integration within the constraints of professional comfort and does not therefore achieve full integration. The implication of this view is that any gradual change is seen as a stumbling block rather than a building block in the development of new services. In his view the speed of change posed by the development of integrated services can often underestimate the degree of working-through required to achieve meaningful change and can lead to an over-emphasis on "getting things done", avoiding the necessary debate and productive conflict being dealt with and leaving groups marginalized and disengaged. Within a systemic framework, in order to achieve the sorts of change that are meaningful and productive, one needs to develop local narratives through partnership in order to really have integrated services, which cannot be achieved without some autonomous local decision-making. For many on the course, participants identifying the key players and their views of why services had developed over time in particular ways was crucial in beginning to develop ideas about how things might be different. This focus on local solutions (Campbell, Coldicott, & Kinsella, 1994) assumes leadership styles that enable careful listening to the individual narratives that make up organizational culture and to attend to those that are not yet being heard.

Constructed realities

Understanding an organization as a system is about understanding the many contexts and meanings people use to govern their behaviour. Systems exist for a purpose, and this creates the overall context and gives meaning to the activity that takes place. It is a crucial task for managers to be alert to the variety of meanings that influence both themselves as managers and the staff they are involved with. An organization's culture can be thought of as the sets of individual understandings across all staff which concern meanings and values. Within a systemic framework the system is a collection of many realities built up through the myriad interactions people have at work. For each individual these result in a set of meanings that need to be congruent with explicit aims and values of the whole organization to produce overall coherence. It is, of course, not possible for espoused aims and values alone to achieve this—they have to be manifest in the behaviour and decisions of management. How often do we hear of lofty principles that are contradicted in practice? This was a particular problem for one educational psychologist who had the task of developing and implementing an inclusion policy for the borough. Despite a series of consultations and apparent agreement, the final policy was not followed, and local practices continued. It was not until he stepped back and identified a wider range of key players and explored their views both about inclusion, their various roles in relation to this, and the effect any changes would have on these that a better fit between a management task and those on the ground was possible.

Meanings attributed to events do not arise spontaneously but are constructed by the individual, who acts as an observer with any interaction of which he or she is a part. Through this, each idea is open to revision. This active observation is rarely neutral, and it is likely to be a driver for a range of ideas and anxieties about the present and the future. This is particularly true at times of change. We will attend to the observations that fit our preoccupations about the beliefs and behaviours of others and our own position or status. This was demonstrated by the example above of the educational psychologist who had only considered his role and task in relation to others in his service. The aim of systemic thinking is to clarify some of the influences and the ways they lead to particular constructions of reality—that is, why we believe individuals behave the way they do. This is again an essential understanding for managers, since they have the ultimate authority and power that determine how the organization responds. It is not a matter of the manager getting it right—there is rarely a "truth" in organizational life that everyone will sign up to. The manager is inextricably part of the feedback loops that connect all parts of the organization. The manager as observer is part of the process.

Observer position

Within the course we run at the Tavistock Clinic, we aim to enable managers to observe levels of meaning they are influenced by and to understand why these meanings lead to particular interpretations and consequent behaviour. By taking this "observer" position they become aware of the various influences on them and the ways in which they influence others. This is achieved on the course in a number of ways: by presenting to colleagues and listening to alternative descriptions; by asking questions during their work discussions and in their management roles, rather than giving views; and by generating and listening to feedback. It is hoped that the process will facilitate the creation of new ways of understanding behaviour, leading to new feedback loops. This is particularly important for managers who are also a part of the systems they are attempting to observe, understand, and manage. The manager referred to earlier brought for consultation her dilemma in having managerial responsibility to collect data about the service; she, like her staff, felt suspicious of the value of the task and deeply ambivalent about completing it. Through conversation she linked her lack of commitment to the task—which she was able to trace back to earlier experiences of misused data—to her team's suspicion and lack of cooperation. She was also aware that her team had experienced problems in sharing information when their work had been viewed as ineffective and poorly managed. Now she was facing a situation in which data collection was a crucial communication tool with commissioners. Through the consultation process she chose to take up a role that would place her and her team in better contact and communication with the external environment and create an efficient feedback loop that would enable them to develop more meaningful data rather than defend against collecting it. The team worked together exploring their beliefs and fears about the role of data collection and how their service was evaluated. They then worked with the information officer of the trust to develop an appropriate data set. When reflecting on the task, this manager thought that one of the effects of this exercise was that the team developed a stronger shared identity and a positive position within the wider trust.

Many managers found it helpful to consider all the influences from previous roles that they have played in both their professional and personal life that influence and are influenced by their current role as manager. For many, these were in conflict with the external political discourses that are influencing and shaping services. The economic drivers for health care provision can never be underestimated. One cannot disagree with the proposal to improve access and availability of psychological therapies. However, one might be less enthusiastic about the underlying subjugated narrative of therapy to return people to work, and the simplistic definitions and proposed solutions for what can be very complex psychological difficulties. Social constructionism (Burr, 1995) suggests that our social world is constructed actively by the interactions between and within groups of people, creating a set of ideas or shared beliefs that influence our behaviour. Within these social realities there are dominant ideas and explanations that shape our thinking and experience. Not all stories, however, have equal status, and some may become peripheral or subjugated.

This was a particular issue for one manager who was given the task of developing a psychological therapy strategy for adult mental health services. For her, the dominant discourse around how the high investment in professional identity gets played out in different contexts was crucial in helping deal with some of the competition between professionals for resources, particularly where there were differences in models/philosophies of care. The services she was asked to bring together into one strategy had developed in very different ways. Community services were proud of not being medically led and were viewed as working flexibly but with little accountability. In contrast, some of the more acute services viewed themselves as dealing with complex difficulties with a need for high levels of psychiatric input. There were a number of therapy providers, with no relationship with one another or clarity about their roles and functions. There were multiple entry points into services, with access and availability being inequitable. The community services expressed fears about future services being medically led, as they believed this would undermine professional identity and autonomy in relation to their work and wanted to sit outside the strategy, and initially the child psychiatrist in another service withdrew from the consultation. In her view, if an organization loses sight of its core business and only becomes submerged within the domain of emotional relationship, it is likely to stop developing in a current context. With this in mind, and with the support of the director of mental health services, she set up a series of meetings with all those involved, addressing four key questions:

1. What might be the main psychological characteristics of the new organization?
2. What might it be like to work in such an organization?
3. What dilemmas might be faced in the new context?
4. What are the implication for their theory and practice?

She also addressed these questions for herself during the consultation process. The most helpful idea for her in grappling with her task was that of subjugated or marginalized narratives (Burr, 1995). By exploring these with a variety of staff groups, she discovered a wider range of ideas and opinions than she had initially anticipated. Of particular importance were new ideas about leadership, such as transformational leadership (Metcalf & Metcalf, 2005), where different stakeholders are actively involved in developing new ideas, contributions, and positions; and distributed leadership, where there is a devolution of decision-making at all levels in the organization (Huffington, James, & Armstrong, 2004). These enabled her to invite all the stakeholders to join her in developing a strategy. Central to this was her capacity to take an observer position. This enabled her to identify the diversity of opinion and the challenges that arose as individuals and staff groups positioned themselves in different ways and at different times in relation to the questions and dilemmas she posed (Campbell & Grønbæk, 2006). Appreciating difference as a resource and as a springboard for change was central to the process. By reflecting on her own disappointment and disillusionment with management in the past, she was able to see new ideas of leadership emerging, as described above.

For all the managers I have worked with, the opportunity for time to reflect with peers or in some form of supervisory/mentoring relationship was crucial.

Role and the idea of fit

I and others have written elsewhere about how in any organization people are in a position of trying to balance their individual needs, ideas, and beliefs with those of the group and the wider context (Campbell, Coldicott, & Kinsella, 1994; Harris, 2005). We all work for a variety of reasons—income, personal satisfaction, status, and so on. When personal gains are met through work, the employee will be satisfied and continue to work for the good of the organization. However, when the organizational task is unsatisfying or in conflict with individual needs, individuals may become less motivated to cooperate in this. Many managers on the course found that the idea of taking up a role in the organization was helpful in trying to explore this idea of fit. However, many managers expressed a concern that a traditional way in which the role of manager is taken up is to maintain high levels of professional independence and responsibility for individual work within the service. A framework for management that places explicit emphasis on regulating processes rather than on controlling people may serve to allay legitimate anxieties about relationships with authority. This model assumes optimistically that individuals will manage themselves in ways that further the aims of the organization. This model may be less relevant when the organization is a multi-agency one.

Such organizations do not necessarily have a shared view of the core business or primary task, and members may act as if the primary task is to provide for their own satisfaction and needs, particularly when engagement with the task is painful or causes psychological conflict within or between group members. This seemed to be particularly acute for managers in children's services within local authorities where they were facing integration of services and the likelihood of managing and being managed by those from other professional backgrounds and experiences. Many found the idea of taking up a role helpful in exploring some of their difficulties. This is essentially the psychological process of developing an idea in the mind rather than a set of behaviours. It depends upon the person construing what the values, aims, and objectives of the organization are at various levels—the whole, the section of which they are a part, and the individuals with whom they are engaged. This provides the context within which they construct the idea of their own role, which provides the basis for feelings, attitudes, decisions, and actions.

It is of central importance to organizational success that the ideas of role held by staff are complementary and clear. This clarity is provided by well thought-through aims and objectives and values that set up clear organizational boundaries. These enable managers to become persons in role, rather than just persons in the organization. Role clarity provides internal security for staff as well as being the route to creative and imaginative responses to new situations. These ideas are of particular significance to managers, as within this framework it is understood that a system that develops strong role identity for its staff maximizes autonomy and empowerment. Management becomes a process of regulation, monitoring, and support rather than of control. This was certainly true in the example of the manager who was able to work with her staff in developing a more appropriate data set for their service.

However, while components of the system must fit in this way, for creativity to be possible there must also be sufficient difference and diversity among the parts for each to be defined. The system needs to be flexible and responsive to new demands and to be able to adjust to new feedback. It is important to have good fit between person and role. This is influenced by the way the person perceives the aims and objectives of the organization. Similarly, fit is required between roles within the organization that ensure complementarity and synergy. This is perhaps particularly important to bear in mind with the development of multi-agency teams—that is, teams populated by staff not just from different disciplines but also employed by different agencies with different values and cultures. Several course members over recent years have been in posts as leaders and managers of such teams. Most have experienced an implicit, and sometimes an explicit, communication to get on with the task and not explore the tensions experienced within the teams and services they are to lead. An example of how this issue was addressed on the course is the following: Two course members from the same borough interviewed the relevant directors within the borough separately and then together, followed by similar conversations within their services. They focused on the hoped-for outcomes for their teams from management and team members, what these would look like, and the roles required to achieve them. In these conversations they paid particular attention to the potential losses and gains for individuals and each organization. What emerged were differences between the directors about, for example, outcomes and within the teams about how to achieve these, the perceived value placed on different skills, and the degree of autonomy in using these. The result was the directors agreeing to meet the managers together on a regular basis, a greater congruence between those with the vision for and those delivering the services, and greater clarity and agreement about respective roles and their value.

New conversations

Many participants through their mapping of the system and exploring the views of others became aware that many of the situations they were bringing for consultation were those in which underlying beliefs and difficulties were not spoken about or, more commonly, that conversations where anxieties and fears were aired were not shared. Many of the managers I have worked with struggled with the question of how to develop new conversations. Adopting a systemic approach by mapping the system, remaining neutral and curious, and taking up the position of observer and respectful listener were all ways in which participants began to open up new conversations about situations that they and others were feeling stuck with. When able to incorporate the views of others without losing sight of the core task, they were able to see real shifts in the organization.

Within this book, Clare Huffington explores in her chapter the possibility of changing systems by working with an individual. Certainly my experience of working with managers is that using the opportunity to reflect on the system(s) of which they are a part, on their role, and on some of the assumptions held within those particular contexts has enabled quite profound changes to take place (although often not as they might have expected). All spoke of the importance of a shared or at least an understood strategic vision within the organization in order to implement any changes. In order to do this it was important for individuals to see a valued role for themselves and their profession. This is crucial to the idea of fit outlined above. For many, making explicit and examining the dilemmas posed by conflicting beliefs about function, roles, and future directions allowed alternative conversations to take place. This was particularly powerful for one manager who had the task of integrating two professional groups within an education authority. Both felt marginalized and believed that they would achieve the best outcomes for pupils, in mutually contradictory or conflicting ways. For this manager, when meeting with both groups what emerged was a lack of vision of what the new service was aiming to achieve and what the distinctive roles each professional group would play. This tension showed itself in part in disagreements about who should take on a particular piece of casework or project. She chose to explore how each group understood their roles and the management structures to support these, in both individual and group discussions. What emerged was an understanding that current service structures minimized differences between the two professional groups—for example, 11 service meetings were joint. From her exploration this manager concluded that what was needed was a clear vision of the core tasks for the service and how each professional group contributed in their different ways to the whole. Her first step, therefore, was to create two teams in one service, while developing more opportunities for the two groups to work together in practice.

Manager on the boundary—
leadership and management

For an organization to survive it is necessary for managers to be thinking ahead and proactively—that is, to anticipate changes in external contexts and to position the organization in order to address these effectively. In order to be proactive and innovative, feedback is required in both directions—that is, from the external environment and from those within the service. The idea of the manager on the boundary is not a new one. Within a systemic framework the importance of being in good communication with the external environment enables the development of an efficient feedback loop in order to explore and understand beliefs from both within and outside the service. In my experience this has become of increased importance over the years I have been consulting to managers within the public sector.

This role for the manager needs also to reflect differences between individuals within services, as the manager is often in a position of negotiating individual and service needs. As has already been remarked, one manager found this a constant challenge for her in her role as manager. How much more acutely this is felt when there are also new boundaries across cultures in the context of multi-agency work. Systemic thinking, for me, has allowed/enabled the integration of skills required for the maintenance and development of organizations and systems—that is, that of management—and that of leadership—that is, looking forward to the future. Without feedback from managing the task and being proactive in relation to the external context, no organization will survive. In short, it is the balance between stability and change, both of which are necessary—either can be impeding to development or threatening to any sense of survival.

Reflections

I have been struck by the feedback from managers who identify quite dramatic outcomes for their role after exposure to this way of thinking about their role and task. First, they identify an enhanced capacity to plan strategically and take account of the full organizational context in which they work. Second, they report reduced personal anxiety about their responsibility for every small problematic event. Many report that understanding the interconnectedness of systems has enabled them to be more observant of their role and of that of others and to be less reactive. Third, they make more sense of the emotional environment and its impact upon the process of achieving outcomes. Again, many report using their own reactions and those of others as information to help them understand situations. It is difficult to become a systemic manager. The demands that predominate in any management role can be reactive, premised upon simple cause-and-effect thinking, often with no time to allow the greater complexity of systems thinking to take over.

If we wish to develop the capacity of managers to deal with the stresses of ever greater accountability and ever more demanding targets within new contexts, we have to enable them to deal positively with complexity and to base strategy on a deeper under-standing of what is going on in the minds of their staff. This requires opportunities to reflect, to observe at a distance, and to consult with others who share similar challenges. To do this we need to develop a capacity for self-reflection: to continually reflect on what one brings to the process oneself; to reflect on how we as managers are affected by and affect the organization of which we are a part; and to recognize that, for others, our actions have mean-ings that will be affected by their beliefs and attitudes—for exam-ple, about their managers. When I have experienced problems as a manager myself, I often find it is because I have neglected to take into account the position of others—their values, their priorities, what drives them—a common problem in inter-agency working.

The course:
emerging themes

When we considered making this course more multidisciplinary, particularly in the light of the development of more integrated children's services, course members disagreed. The dominant idea was that in order to function effectively, a space to examine ten-sions linked to professional identity was important.

The course has been designed to be manageable within the tight time restrictions that managers face. Therefore, many have requested "top-ups", and small peer consultation groups have developed. There may well be value in training others to deliver the support and consultation being requested locally and in the creation of networks.

Time and time management is a continual theme, particularly in relation to finding time to think and reflect. This is certainly something we will be paying greater attention to in future courses. Similarly biannual short refresher sessions may be of value, as these are groups who have worked together on the course and could pick up thinking with one another quickly. Generally all have appreciated the value of reflecting on process and are anx-ious to maintain this when they leave.

CHAPTER SEVEN

Asymmetric leadership: supporting a CEO's response to turbulence

Philip Boxer & Carole Eigen

Commentary

In the next three chapters, Philip Boxer & Carole Eigen, Simon Western, and Georgina Noakes & Myrna Gower, respectively, tackle systemic approaches to leadership development. The backcloth to these chapters is the far-reaching changes in all organizations brought about by globalization, IT, and an increasingly competitive environment. The consequent need has been to develop strategic alliances and partnership working and greater responsiveness to consumers and clients and to shift more power away from the centre of organizations to the periphery, or "distributed leadership" (Kouzes & Posner, 2003). These changes have demanded that organizations loosen their boundaries to the outside world and also become more agile and responsive. The impact on leaders is that they have had to re-think how to provide direction and purpose to the organization in new circumstances, while at the same time engaging stakeholders both within and outside its boundaries.

Philip Boxer & Carole Eigen describe an approach to consulting to the CEO of the central organization of a federation of religious communities. The presenting problem was that this membership organization was losing members, and this was affecting funding and resources. The CEO had the task of renewing the organization and attracting new members. Boxer & Eigen describe the challenge as one of "asymmetric leadership"—that is, the ability to respond to increasingly differentiated individual members' demands. This requires leadership to be exercised from the point of contact with the member—from the edge of the enterprise in the local communities, not from the centre. It also involves engaging what they call the "tacit sponsoring system" of stakeholders in the enterprise, and bringing to the surface and working with the inevitable conscious and unconscious tensions with the more obvious member system.

In order to do this work, Boxer & Eigen designed a reflexive consultation process that involved an internal shadow consultation group for the CEO. Their task was to make sense of what the CEO was doing as he worked to transform the organization. The group was facilitated by Boxer, with Eigen as his shadow consultant. The map of the consultation process is captured in the idea of "what is going on", or "wigo". This was the exploration and uncovering of layers of meaning by the CEO, members of the consultation group, and the consultants in their different roles.

Boxer & Eigen go on to describe the three phases of the consultation and how they were driven by the internal logic of the consultation process itself. The last phase began as the CEO started to get a grip on a new way of fulfilling his role, which involved sharing and working with others and the creation of a leadership team to build internal connections between the different activities of the organization.

The main contribution of this chapter to the book is in creating a "technology" (the reflexive consultation group, facilitator, and shadow consultant) to explore and examine what was necessary to bring about a leadership transformation. In other circumstances, organizations usually change their leader and/or re-structure, without necessarily working at "what is going on" at a deeper level. This avoids facing some of the deeper systemic issues in terms of creating a bridge between external changes and the consequent challenges to the meaning system in the organization. This is because of the massive anxiety that change

152

tends to create. In avoiding doing this work, organizations pre-
scribe for themselves endless cycles of restructuring and leader-
ship turmoil, as the fundamental issues are never resolved. Boxer
& Eigen's method was also able to contain "systemic annihilation
anxiety" at a time of change, which might otherwise have de-
railed the work.

Their method could easily be adapted for other organizations
facing change. These organizations would need to appreciate the
need for a careful and thoughtful process over a period of time, as
it is not a quick fix but would produce a sustainable solution until
the next leadership challenge had to be faced.   [Eds.]

Twentieth-century approaches to enterprise assumed that leadership had to be exercised ultimately from a single position at the top of a hierarchy. A new challenge is emerging for leadership in the twenty-first century, created by the need to respond to increasingly differentiated individual client demands (Zuboff & Maxmin, 2002). The asymmetric nature of these demands requires leadership to be exercised from the point of contact with the client—that is, from the *edge* of the enterprise (Alberts & Hayes, 2003). The term *asymmetric leadership* describes the nature of the leadership required to hold the client's demands as a central focus and to be able to identify, tolerate, and ultimately address the anxieties that arise as a consequence of the necessity to engage with these asymmetric forms of demand in order to move the goals of the enterprise forward. Such leadership must be exercised by managers collaborating across niche hierarchies in order to contain the significant disturbance created for the enterprise in its attempt to maintain a dynamic alignment with its external environment.

Environmental turbulence may make it necessary to put into question the current structures of governance and customary ways of delivering services in order to mobilize the resources of the enterprise to respond effectively to what the client wants to experience within their own particular context. The enterprise must struggle with the flux in governance structures, individual role definitions, and, ultimately, the challenge to the identity and purpose of the enterprise itself as it attempts to anticipate and respond to new forms of client demand.

This chapter addresses the process by which these issues began to be recognized by a religious movement that sought to discover what was necessary to remain relevant to current and future generations so that it could renew its membership and sustain the financial viability to thrive as a distinct movement. The intervention with the leadership of this movement utilized a reflexive consulting team model developed by Boxer and Eigen (2005). The reflexive process attempts to engage with the issue of how to work with turbulence in order to embrace rapidly expanding client expectations by identifying how the system has been blocking or ignoring what transformations are necessary. Failure to acknowledge what is being ignored in the service of conserving the identity of the movement ultimately endangers the existence of the movement itself. However, the process of confronting turbulence stimulates *systemic annihilation anxiety* that reverberates throughout the movement. The learning system designed to support leadership efforts in this environment requires transformation of leadership style to include "not-knowing" as a primary value for collaborative discovery and future productivity.

Systemic thinking applied to reflexive consultation

A brief tracing of the trajectory of systemic thinking that underpins the particular reflexive model utilized here builds on the seminal work by Miller and Rice (1967b), which addresses the ways in which task and sentient systems could be aligned as a socio-technical system, emphasizing the crucial importance played by the precise definition and control of boundaries. This approach applied open systems theory to the first-order organization of the task system, emphasizing the importance of not isolating any particular causes-and-effects from the circular chains of causality in which they were embedded (McCaughan & Palmer, 1994). Maturana and Varela (1980) observed that systems that were "open" to their environments for the exchange of inputs and outputs at a first-order level could be closed at a second-order level through the way this exchange process is constrained by organization. The innovations of systemic family therapy took this insight a step further by questioning the nature of the second-order closing.

Family systems theorists observed that second-order "closing" was itself symptomatic of a third-order level of organization that determined how repetitive dysfunctional behaviours were formed within a system of meaning that governed family interaction patterns (for the use of this insight in family therapy, see Hoffman, 1981; for its application to enterprises, see Campbell, Coldicott, & Kinsella, 1994). The work of the Milan group within this field was a particular example of an approach to intervening with family systems at the level of their third-order organization in order to bring about change in symptomatic behaviours "stuck" in some form of repetition (Cronen & Pearce, 1985).

The model of reflexive consultation described by Boxer and Eigen (2005) draws on the field of systemic thinking by identifying the first- and second-order organization of the socio-technical system as a *client system* and referring to its third-order organization as the *sponsoring system*. The sponsoring system represents the influence of the "powers that be", whose system of meaning is embodied by the stakeholders in the enterprise and who command obedience tacitly by making certain transactions readily possible while blocking others that remain ignored by the current way of organizing. It is the influence of the tacit sponsoring system that is being identified and ultimately intervened on by the reflexive consulting team so that organizational transformation is possible (see Figure 7.1). *Asymmetric leadership* is the name we give to the form of leadership required to enable the enterprise to adapt its third-order organization so that it can engage with turbulence and stay relevant to client demands. The key linking concept includes a means of identifying and utilizing the ensuing *systemic annihilation anxiety* that is stimulated in the transformation process. It is useful to examine the nature of systemic annihilation anxiety and its relationship to hierarchy as a defence, including the challenge of the *primary risk* to the enterprise of choosing the wrong primary task (Hirschhorn, 1997).

Defences against systemic annihilation anxiety

The function of hierarchy within an enterprise is to determine what is to be paid attention to and what is to be ignored—that is, the model implicit in how the enterprise engages in those tasks crucial to its continuing viability. Hierarchy is also acting as a means of containing individuals' defences against their own personal anxiety. A person's relationship to his or her role within a hierarchy provides him or her with a means of limiting personal anxiety (Menzies, 1959). The classic example is the nurse holding onto the professional notion of her role in order to avoid becoming overwhelmed by being personally open to the suffering of her patients. The double challenge presented by asymmetric forms of demand at once puts the hierarchical business model into question, while at the same time challenging the enterprise to develop new lateral models in response to new forms of demand. This exposes the enterprise to *primary risk*, "the risk of choosing the wrong primary task, that is, a task that ultimately cannot be managed" (Hirschhorn, 1997, p. 3). If we consider the hierarchy to be an "organizational object" in its own right, rather than simply a construction of those working within it (Armstrong, 2004), then it is possible to speak of the hierarchy as a defence against primary risk.

The nature of turbulent environments is such that what constitutes primary risk cannot be defined independently of the dynamics of the environment, so that the efficacy of this organizational object as a defence is itself continually being questioned. Individuals within the enterprise experience systemic anxiety as a consequence of the potential demise of the hierarchy of roles itself, and with it the support it provides for their identities. In these terms, the hierarchy itself gets conserved as a defence against the systemic anxiety associated with failing to manage its primary risk. Given that this primary risk is the danger that the identity of the enterprise itself will be annihilated, this raises the question of the kind of leadership needed to stay viable under these conditions.

Contrasting leadership styles

Two styles of leadership are associated with enterprises in stable environments where business models are not in question. The first leadership style is represented by the approach, "I am the way, follow me", suggesting an identification with the person of the char-ismatic leader. The second style is represented by the approach, "Follow what I tell you because I know what you don't yet know". This is characteristic of hierarchical organizations where there are "unwritten rules" and the organizational knowledge is built over years of careful progression upwards. The standards are defined by which roles are to be performed, and one must always check upwards to find out "how things are done here".

However, in circumstances where every situation presents its own unique challenge, what the leader knows can get in the way of recognizing what needs to become known. A third style of lead-ership therefore becomes necessary, one in which the leader takes the position that "While we are not able to know by using our existing ways to consider this problem, we can work to discover a new way if we learn from the nature of the situation itself". Examples of this kind of leadership can be found among the best professionals, therapists, doctors, consultants, those who are pre-pared to address the particular condition as they are in the process of encountering the demand. This is *asymmetric leadership*, because its authority is not based on what is already known, but on their engagement with the situation itself.

The following sections offer a practical example of the way we have built upon these concepts to intervene with a client system that is confronting these issues as it struggles for its continued existence in the midst of a turbulent environmental condition that is threatening its existence into the future. We describe the client situation as it presented itself and the learning system we con-structed within the religious movement to help move the trans-formational process forward.

Description of the client system

The client system was the central organization of a federation of religious communities spanning the country, each one pay-ing local subscriptions and electing a Chairman and Board of Governors, and each Board in turn appointing an ordained person to minister to the community's needs. Nationally, the membership numbered many thousands, and the local communities appointed the central organization to represent their collective interests, to provide shared services, and to agree matters of common policy and direction. These services included such things as primary and secondary education, youth work, fund raising, employment advice, and external relations. The central organization had the same structures of governance as existed for each of the communities, except that its income was derived both from its own fundraising activities as well as from a levy paid by the local organizations. Also, its Chairman and Board of Governors were elected by representatives of the local organizations, not by the members themselves. In this context, it was not surprising that the CEO appointed to lead the movement was himself ordained. He had not only to articulate the larger vision of a religious movement that could recover its sense of vitality and expansion, but also to do it in a way that could encourage well-wishers to invest in that movement's future. To achieve this, he had to be identified unquestionably with the core mission of the movement.

The presenting problem

The difficulty facing the movement was one shared by many membership organizations: losing members while competing for time and attention, against a backcloth of changing expectations, shifting demographics, and a generation gap. Not only was this gradual attrition of members affecting the balance and health of the communities, but it was also affecting their funding. Recent attempts to reverse this trend had not been as effective as hoped, and the central organization had appointed a Chief Executive to bring about a renewal of the movement. His brief was to honour the strengths of the existing local organizations, to work in support of the renewal of the communities themselves, and to reach out to entirely new ways of attracting and working with new members. At the same time, the pressures on funding meant that the central organization had to re-evaluate the services it was able to provide to the local organizations.

The challenge of the case

The challenge of the case was that, at the same time as retrenching and redefining the role of the central organization, its leadership also had to reach out to the local organizations and engage with them in a different way as part of its mission to renew its relationship with both existing and prospective members. In this way the actual demands it faced were *asymmetric* to its usual way to recognize what its members expected from the religious movement.

This was a *double challenge* (Boxer, 2004), in which the meaning and purpose of the movement was being questioned at the same time as it sought to act meaningfully and purposefully. The double nature arose because the movement needed to change the way it related to a changing environment at the same time as it sought to redefine the value that could be gained by the services that were provided centrally to the communities. The slowing of growth provided the imperative to face this challenge. In effect, the movement could no longer assume that its model of how to relate to the "world views" of its members and potential members was appropriate, because it could no longer assume that the members' world views were symmetrical with its knowledge of that world.

The reflexive consultation process enabled the CEO to take up a place from which to question the model within which he himself was working. In the original encounter with the CEO, it had been agreed that an external consultant could certainly not know any better than he how to meet his double challenge. The consultation process would therefore have to be one that enabled the CEO himself to work out how to meet the challenge on behalf of the movement. The religious nature of the movement's role in its members' lives made it easier to establish the need for a reflexive process that required an explicit and shared agenda for learning in which neither consultant nor the CEO could claim to "know best" (Boxer & Palmer, 1994).

The learning system design:
a reflexive consultation process

The learning system that was designed to support the leadership efforts of the CEO of this religious movement combines psychodynamic, systemic, and group relations concepts. The basic premise is that an interacting shadow consulting system can be induced to reproduce the dynamics of the larger membership system when it responds to and interacts with the CEO. If these dynamics are encouraged to emerge in the shadow consulting system and are carefully observed and reflected upon by its members with the facilitation of the outside consultant, then useful hypotheses can be formed that have the potential to surface unspoken obstacles to the achievement of the goals of the movement. The recognition of ignored dynamics that thwart change may guide the direction and focus of the leadership so that the genuine needs and specific demands of the members for whom the movement exists to serve may be addressed more effectively (Boxer & Eigen, 2005).

The design innovation in this particular learning system involved forming an *internal shadow consultation group* from individuals currently working under contract to or within the client system. The roles of these individuals were taken from a "diagonal" so that there were no direct hierarchical relationships within the group or between its members and the CEO. Thus four people were chosen by the CEO to work with him to represent the variety of views and influences within the movement about the nature of its work: a member of the Board of Governors for the central organization, a consultant working with some of the local communities on their renewal, and two ordained persons, one from the central educational organization and one ministering to the needs of the local ministers.

The task of the consultation group was to attend to its different ways of making sense of what the CEO was doing as he worked to transform the movement. This interactive process was directly facilitated by Boxer, with Eigen acting as his shadow consultant. The goal of this facilitation was to enable the group to notice what was being avoided or was difficult to surface in its own dynamics as it struggled with its task. In this way, the group confronted itself with the question of what it was unable to speak about among its own members. The assumptions about the primary risk of engaging with the wrong primary task were to be found in that which was being avoided, and they surfaced obliquely in the mirrored obstacles to expression arising within the consultation group. By paying attention to the gaps in what was able to be expressed, the nature of the primary risk was made present.

The theoretical model that underlies the structure of the process is briefly outlined below, to enable the "map" used to guide the contract and method of facilitation to become more apparent.

The theoretical map of the consultation

Three concepts underpin the theoretical model of organizational transformation that guide our approach and method of facilitation. The first two concepts are derived from systemic thinking: these include the effects of the socio-technical system that is embodied in the *client* system, and its third-order *sponsoring system*, with particular unspoken assumptions about what constitutes a primary risk (Figure 7.1).

The third concept links systemic thinking to psychoanalysis and describes the nature of *what-is-going-on* (*"wigo"*) in relation to the enterprise on an unconscious level. Numerous accounts of what was happening in and to the movement emerged during the course of the work of the consultation group. These accounts often differed in their form and content, which reflected the different interests and perspectives of their observers. The concept of

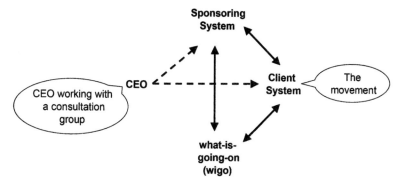

Figure 7.1.   The CEO's relationship to the enterprise

wigo is a way of referring to a "beyond" of those accounts that is never fully captured by the accounts themselves. (This "beyond" is the Lacanian "Real", to be distinguished from "reality" which is how it appears to the client and sponsoring systems. See, for example, "Tuché and Automaton", in Lacan, 1977). Thus, however hard members of the client system—who are represented in this case by the consultation group—worked at becoming conscious of what was going on in the movement, the assumption was that they would always be limited by the way the sponsoring system mediated their actions, and there would always be something of what was going on that remained unconscious or "beyond" their knowledge of it.

The relationships between these dynamic forces that mediate the functioning of the system and give it its unique identity are represented by the three positions that are shown in Figure 7.1. The position of the CEO working in conjunction with the consultation group is indicated as a fourth position from which the nature of the client and sponsoring systems are being observed and articulated. No direct relationship to *wigo* is possible from the fourth position because *wigo* is always mediated by the dynamics of the other two positions.

The model enables us to address the double challenge inherent in the nature of organizational transformation, in that it provides a way to direct attention to what forms of change have to take place:

» within the client system in relation to the demands arising from *wigo*
» within the sponsoring system itself in relation to what forms of demand from the external environment may or may not be recognized by the client system.

The contract and its facilitation

The structure of the contract with the facilitator of this learning system involved: consultation to the dynamics between the internal consultation group and the CEO, which included responding to what was surfaced by the CEO as he worked within the movement; consultation to the exchanges that remained "private" to the interactions between the consultation group members; and consultation to what was said by the consultation group to the CEO in the form of a group intervention. The reflexive contract required that *all* parties involved be prepared to question their own prior assumptions and to work with the discomfort of not-knowing— external consultants and facilitators included. The dynamics that emerged between members of the shadow consultation team provided evidence from which to build hypotheses about what was going on in the larger movement (diagrammed in Figure 7.1 as the "client system") as it engaged with the CEO's efforts.

The process was based on monthly face-to-face meetings during a period of nine months; in addition, the consultation group met on its own, as well as with the CEO. The content of the meetings revolved around a journal kept by the CEO along with any other material he chose to circulate to the consultation group. These monthly meetings took place within the context of frequent weekly e-mail exchanges about *wigo*, both within the group and between the group and the CEO. The discipline was that group members only commented on what was raised by the CEO in these exchanges, and the exchanges within the group related to what each considered significant in what was being raised by the CEO and how their views on this differed from one another.

The model in Figure 7.1 allows us to propose that every communication carried with it its own sponsoring assumptions, and every communication about what was going on (*wigo*) pointed towards its own "beyond" about which it could not speak. The facilitation process was about working ceaselessly to make as much of this accessible to the consultation group as was possible.

Logical timing of the process

The process was divided into three logical phases such that the precise timing of the transitions between them depended on the emergent learning of the CEO and consultation group. (These phases are based on the Lacanian concept of "logical time" that appears in "Logical Time and the Assertion of Anticipated Certainty", in Lacan, 2006.)

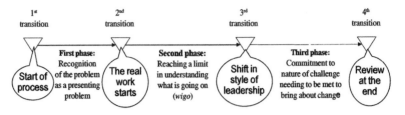

Figure 7.2.   The timing of the three phases

The process started from the presenting problem, with the transitions being characterized as outlined in Figure 7.2.

» The first phase *ended* when the CEO realized that the particular way in which he understood the presenting problem was a symptom of something more profoundly problematic that had not yet been clearly identified.

» The second phase went on until the CEO became aware that a particular limit had been reached in his current way of understanding what was going on; there was something fundamentally missing in his understanding.

» The third phase *started* when the CEO realized that the particular form of leadership needed to make the necessary changes required him to find new ways of enabling people to feel authorized to respond to the demands on the movement.

It can take time to integrate the realization that emerges at the end of the second phase, and therefore a gap was expected between the ending of the second phase and the beginning of the third. The process as a whole ended when the CEO was far enough into the third phase to be able to recognize what he had learned, a choice that the CEO had to make within the agreed overall timeframe. In order to understand the nature of the "something that was fundamentally missing", it is necessary to look more closely at how the process unfolded.

The first phase

The first phase revolved around the preparation for a meeting with key members of the communities, in which what was at stake was the CEO's core document for how the transformation itself was to be achieved. This was formulated in terms of a number of projects addressing different aspects of the movement's development, together with an account of the fundamental challenge the movement faced—namely, to what end was it to be agreed that it was ultimately there for its members. The CEO had taken the membership challenge and broken it down into projects so that each could be run independently of the others, delegable as a whole task in itself. The questions remained, what was the ultimate purpose of the movement in the lives of the members, and what was needed to coordinate across these projects to ensure that they all came together successfully?

The catch that emerged at the meeting with key members of the communities was that while the CEO had the responsibility to bring all the pieces together as a whole, it was not clear that he had the authority or funding to make the projects themselves happen. Nor was it clear to what extent there was a commitment among the membership for making the projects happen. This again raised the whole question of what forms of collaboration the members were prepared to engage in, and to what end. This was exactly the question that the CEO had been appointed to resolve. As one member of the consultation group put it:

> "The challenge is, once you have arrived at the space which holds vision, how do you do the leadership bit which empowers/enables/demands of people to move forward with you. We have moved into the doing phase. A phase where we are going to be judged not on the clarity of our thinking and the exquisiteness of our metaphors, but on whether we do the job. This is your challenge of leadership right now. Not to get up on your horse and ride off ahead of the people, but to ensure that you have the right people with you to do the work, to share the load with you."

The first phase ended at the point where it was realized that there was something fundamentally missing in the CEO's way of understanding what would energize and drive the work of the movement.

"When we started, my fantasy was that a consultant could come in and sort out the issue of relationships between staff, lay leaders, and ministers. We have been on a huge journey since then—trying to identify the real problem, trying to find a structure to move us forward. We have made a lot of progress in those areas but we now seem to be back at issues of 'How do we all work together in order to realize the vision we have set within the structure we have created?' and 'How do we all work together, relationally rather than instrumentally, to develop the ideas and their implementation?'"

The second phase

This realization plunged the consultation group into the second phase, which felt much more open-ended and much messier. They had to struggle again with what was really going on, and what would be a sufficient basis for securing collaboration among the members. What had been realized were the limitations of the CEO's authority, the other side of which was, what would authorize what needed doing? The day-to-day activities of the communities had become split off from the questions of the movement:

"We are a Movement that has utterly separated the running of the local communities from the religious and the lay from ministers. All of this highlights that what I am suggesting is a real shock for both sides, and it is probably so shocking that most people don't realize it—particularly the ministers."

The consultation group had to work hard during the second phase. Each individual surfaced his or her own critical perspective on the CEO's journal of *wigo*, expressing it always in relation to the CEO's position. *Thus while the CEO was listening to the needs of the movement, the consultation group was listening to the way the CEO listened.* Within the process itself, the distinction was held between "personal stuff" and views that could be read as expressing something on behalf of the sponsoring system. It became possible to separate out distinctly different ways of looking at *wigo* by working at this distinction. This was reflected in the questions that emerged:

» What small and practical steps can we take so that we don't get distracted and the larger picture can be left to take care of itself?

» How are we to restore faith with the fundamentals of religious identity so that we can move forward?

» What is it about what is going on that makes us all feel so fragmented and makes us experience such difficulty in working with each other's positions?

» What is it that we want from our ministers in all of this?

» How do we open up and extend learning beyond that of our ministers?

It became apparent that the group remained absolutely silent about the question of the demands of the members on the movement. By "demand" is here meant some way in which a person experienced a need that they understood as being religious in nature and that was capable of being satisfied in some way by the services offered by the movement. It was as if the nature of this demand was self-evident, while at the same time the consultation group appeared to have no way of speaking about it, even though this was the rationale for the movement itself. Again, a comment from a member of the consultation group:

"I have a hunch that one of the great injustices done to our ministers and, via this injustice, now to our communities via their unfulfilled frustration and anger is that the traditional roles were changed, and new, unrealistic roles were created. From clear expectations of ministers to be interpreters and teachers, our ministers were asked to be social workers, psychologists, community professionals, teachers, managers, and so forth. I feel strongly that the way to begin dealing with this is to come clean about it and to stop pretending that we just need to tweak curricula or give secretarial support."

The second phase ended somewhere around the point at which the CEO realized that the harder he tried, the less things seemed to move. "Trying harder" was caricatured as kissing frogs in the hope that they would be transformed as a result. But the hard work of the consultation group was bringing them nowhere near the question of into what the frogs were supposed to be transforming.

The third phase

The experience of working back-and-forth with differences in the second phase brought the CEO to the realization that what was fundamentally missing was implicated in the way he was fulfilling his own role on behalf of the movement:

> "There are issues of relationality that need working on . . . the realization that I don't have to know all of the answers . . . how key people are empowered and given legitimacy . . . and my really giving other people space and responsibility so that they have a real stake in what is going on and I stop killing myself."

The fact that the work had entered the third phase began to show itself at the end of a long session with the consultation group in which it recognized the extent to which its members did not speak to each other about their different understandings of what constituted the role of a minister, nor about the relationship between this role and the governance and structure of the movement itself. Expressed as a way of managing the primary risk, the feared trauma of disagreeing over the role of a minister led the group to be unable to address this issue. This silence deprived the movement of a way of understanding how it should respond to the differing needs of individuals "at the edge".

In working on why this might be so, it was agreed that it was the individual's personal struggle for meaning and purpose that lay at the root of the latent demands on the movement. But it was exactly this relationship that was defined as not being relevant to the work of the minister, precisely because it got in the way of his being able to hold the traditional role and, indeed, could take forms that would be very challenging for the minister himself/herself. Here was the sponsoring system organizing what could be spoken of and what needed to be ignored.

When the group fed this gap back to the CEO, it became evident that something had changed in the way it was understanding *wigo*. It had been difficult to identify what needed to surface within the group, and it was doubly difficult for the CEO to hold the group to address what it was trying so hard to ignore! Instead, he was colluding with the group to hide from it in order to manage his own anxiety: if he did not know what the group did not know, what kind of leader was he?

In presenting this gap/lack in the group's own ability to speak about what was going on, the CEO was enabled to contain the group in relation to its own not-knowing and establish for himself a different relationship to the challenge he faced:

"So huge is the pressure on me that I struggle to get out from under. It is hard ... to stop behaving in the way that I currently deal with pressure by trying to deal on my own with everything that is in front of me, in order to share and work with others."

Here was the transformation in his leadership style that was needed to take up the double challenge facing the movement.

The next cycle of work

The CEO had to separate out the delegation of management from the challenge of meeting the membership demands on the movement. This meant challenging the previously unquestioned assumption that everyone already knew what the ordained leadership needed to be doing. Once that question became mobilized, it pointed to other questions that in turn raised the levels of anxiety once again and led to a new cycle of work. The immediate practical result of this intervention was the establishment of a provisional leadership team to begin to build the internal connections between the different activities. The activities had typically not been linked, and certainly not linked to supporting the new direction for the movement. The next consultation cycle surfaced this need to separate out the leadership of the movement from the leadership of the service organization supporting the movement. This in turn led to changes in governance structures beginning to be addressed, with a director being appointed to lead the central organization, and to the re-emergence of the theological question underlying the movement: what constituted ministry in support of individuals' search for meaning and purpose?

Discussion: confronting environmental turbulence, primary risk, and anxiety in this client system

To say that the environment is turbulent is to say that it has a life of its own: it does not conform to the expectations held by the movement, and therefore it behaves asymmetrically. Thus it could no longer be assumed that people would keep joining the communities and taking up its traditions as they entered into adulthood, married, formed families, and got old. It was necessary to ask questions that had never been asked before about how the movement had to change to meet their needs. The turbulence was experienced as a kind of fragmenting and splintering across a myriad of activities responding to different individuals' and communities' needs that was both overwhelming and unaffordable.

The primary risk being managed was the avoidance of the trauma of loss of identification with the movement as it has been historically defined. The place of the ordained person had been the guarantor of this historically defined role for the community. Therefore, to question this role was to question the very formation of the community itself. But the trauma of loss of identity and identification was gradually being overlaid with another potential trauma, the death of the community itself through the loss of active engagement from its present and future members. In effect, the nature of the primary risk to the movement had changed. The defences against anxiety of its members locked in the first implicit assumption about primary risk in terms of the loss of individual identity. But this was being challenged by a present danger defining a new formulation of primary risk—namely, the loss of active engagement with the community itself. The work of the consultation group made this contradiction apparent in a way that enabled them to "own" it in their own working.

The structure of the process was effective in holding the systemic annihilation anxiety. The subsequent intervention with the provisional leadership team was also effective for as long as its identity remained provisional. The point of difficulty arose when the issues emerging from its work had to be acted upon. Here, there was a hiatus and a pause as the "old" and the "new" views of what was needed had to square up to each other, and decisions had to be made over how to resolve their differences, a process in which the passing of time itself was a powerful influence.

It is difficult to overstate the significance of "getting under the skin" of the resistance to change in the movement and of giving the CEO purchase on the "real" process of transformation. The fact that it has not been a quick result is perhaps not surprising, but there is no doubt that the transformation has a direction, momentum, and depth to it that it would not otherwise have had.

Conclusion

The need for enterprises to work directly in relation to the individual client's experience is by no means restricted to religious movements. Apart from the obvious need of professional service organizations of all kinds to do this, even manufacturing businesses are discovering the value in supporting the experience of the end-user. Taking "power to the edge" of the enterprise in this way requires exceptional levels of flexibility in the enterprise's infrastructures that are very difficult to sustain. But the core difficulty is to lead asymmetrically—that is, in a way that can hold the client's experience at the centre of the enterprise's work.

Other applications of this reflexive consultation model have varied in the constituting of the consultation group, the position of the client, and the nature of the enterprise, but the essential elements have remained the same, with the emergent logical timing of the phases being their common feature. The basic premise of the process is that an interacting shadow consulting team will parallel the dynamics of the larger system and that if these dynamics are carefully observed and reflected upon by the team members, they will allow useful hypotheses to emerge that reveal the unspoken obstacles that the enterprise is defending itself against knowing.

One of the difficulties with this method, when deployed within more overtly commercial forms of enterprise, is that greater attention has to be given to the particular infrastructure challenges inherent in responding to asymmetric forms of demand. Thus the technical nature of the work involved in the religious movement was much easier to grasp than, for example, in health care, even though the effects of the sponsoring system are no less great. Given this *caveat* and the challenges it presents for managing the agility of complex systems of systems, the reflexive method provides an effective way of enabling the CEO to develop a capability for such leadership and to establish the particular form it needs to take.

Much attention has been given to training leaders to cope with the emergent demands of this twenty-first-century period of rapid and turbulent change. The concepts and methodology of reflexive consultation provide an approach to leadership training, based on systemic and psychoanalytic understanding of the relationship to not-knowing. This understanding is not just deeply meaningful and personally gratifying, but pragmatically necessary to managing the level of change being demanded by increasingly asymmetric environments.

CHAPTER EIGHT

Democratizing strategy: towards distributed leadership

Simon Western

Commentary

In the second of the three chapters addressing systemic approaches to leadership development, Simon Western describes his consultation to a partner-based organization established to deliver leadership excellence in the further education and learning and skills sector in the United Kingdom. The purpose of the work was to develop a "radically inclusive approach" to strategic planning.

Influenced by structural family therapy and a historical systemic perspective on the Quakers' use of distributed leadership, Western worked with the CEO, firstly in the role of coach. Together they devised ways to change the organizational culture so that others could take up a leadership role in strategic planning. Western describes this as a blend of "paternal containment"—that is, creating spaces in the organizational architecture—and "maternal containment"—using these spaces for creativity and reflection to take place.

They created Strategic Forums for different groups of staff in order to enable networking, open communication, and creativity.

Western facilitated these using various techniques influenced by systemic practice—for example, a "free-association matrix", peer consultancy, a systems movement game, and network mapping. All of these were designed to challenge usual ways of thinking and to stimulate creativity. The Strategic Forums proved to be a powerful means of engaging groups of staff and developing shared ideas and innovative suggestions for improving practice. The forums were brought together in an Annual Dialogue event for the whole system where all the ideas were gathered in the form of an emergent strategy for the organization. The intervention was highly successful in helping the whole organization to integrate and operate more effectively internally as well as to achieve, or even over-achieve, on its delivery targets.

Organizations usually approach the development of strategy by the CEO and leadership team doing the work, with perhaps a nod to consultation by asking groups of staff to comment on ideas they have developed. It is brave and unusual for the entire process of strategic planning to be devolved to the staff of the organization itself in the manner Western describes. It required the CEO to genuinely relinquish power and to trust in the paternal and maternal containment created by her, with Western working together with her. It would have been interesting to hear how the organization agreed the strategy from the output of the Annual Dialogue—for example, which ideas were supported and which were not?

Unlike Boxer & Eigen's chapter, we do not hear much about the sponsoring system representing the demands of the external environment, which might have required the internal democratization of strategy development. This would have been a useful addition to the account of this consultation.   [Eds.]

This chapter describes an intervention that aimed to take a radically inclusive approach to strategic planning in an organization in the education sector in the United Kingdom. The intervention aimed to maximize participation in the strategic process and, through this process, help to build a culture that was emancipatory—a culture where employees had increasing agency to influence change. To achieve this, my client and I set out to engage the whole system and to encourage a holistic and connected appreciation of the organization. Finally, the aim was to take a spatial look at the organizational architecture and create new "thinking spaces" that would become internalized and part of the culture for the future.

The systemic theory
that influenced my approach

My approach to this particular intervention draws on two sources:

1. Structural family therapy theory and practice.
2. A historical systemic perspective on the Quakers' use of dispersed leadership and emergent strategy (Western, 2005).

Structural family therapy theory and practice

As a family therapist working in the 1980s and 1990s, I was heavily influenced by the ideas of Salvador Minuchin and structural family therapy (Minuchin, 1974). Now that I am Director of Coaching at Lancaster University, I have been teaching a systemic coaching module and draw upon structural family therapy theory and practice to describe how to apply systems theory into coaching practice. Systems thinking has been applied to management thinking and practice for some time, with Peter Senge (1990) being its most prominent figure. However, Senge has his critics, who highlight some of the more general challenges for systems thinking. For example, Senge's work idealizes community and over-plays the importance of dialogue without adequately addressing power (Coopey, 1995). Power is structurally hidden within discourses and normative assumptions, behaviours, and organizational culture. Dialogue alone does not challenge the power elites that will continue to replicate existing norms—for example, all-male boardrooms. Other criticisms of his work are that it reads well but is not easily translated into practice (partly due to the power critique), nor is there evidence that his writing has had a great impact in the field (Fielding, 2001; Frank, 2001).

In an attempt to address these criticisms, I draw on the experience of how structural family therapists managed to use systemic theory in practice and confronted head-on issues of power imbalances—for example, within slum settings—and how this impacted on families (Minuchin, 1974). Structural family therapy brings a coherent theoretical framework that arose from practice.

If one part of the system presents as dysfunctional—for example, if an individual is anorexic—the therapist tries to understand how different parts of the system interact to maintain the state of equilibrium that keeps the individual anorexic. This contrasts with a medical model of simply treating the individual as a medical or psychological problem. The systems explored are multiple: the individual's biological and psychodynamic system; the extended family psychological and social systems; and the other social systems—schools, neighbours, friends—that interact and maintain stasis. Each individual/family in therapy must be understood as unique and "*situated*" within a network of systems of action and influence. It is the therapist's work to unravel this network and restructure it in a functional way through working with the family. There are no universal rules, only ways of exploring each system, with the family drawing on its own resources. Minuchin and Fishman (1981) counselled against the dangers of a technique-driven theory of family therapy:

> If the therapist becomes wedded to technique, remaining a craftsman, his contact with patients will be objective, detached, and clean, but also superficial [and] manipulative for the sake of personal power, and ultimately not highly effective. [Minuchin & Fishman, 1981, p. 1]

There is a symbiotic relationship between the family and therapist, whereby the therapist joins the family system and becomes like a "distant relative" in the work of changing the system to enable new patterns to emerge.

A particular structural issue is the spatial element in family dynamics—for example, enmeshment (over-involvement) and disengagement (avoiding emotional contact). All families and their subsystems move between either one of these extremes, and, if they go too far, they become stuck and unable to resolve conflict or adapt to change. If a family presents with a rigid family structure, it might be too tightly organized and enmeshed in its emotional ties. An individual may then fight for some autonomy by, say, controlling his or her body weight, as it seems to be the person's last refuge of independence. The therapist's role would be to "unbalance" the family system and "destructure the rigid boundaries before restructuring takes place" (Goldenberg & Goldenberg, 1996, p. 190), allowing autonomy to be gained in other, less destructive ways.

The structural family therapist also focuses on hierarchy and power relationships, establishing generational boundaries—for example, ensuring that parents take on appropriate parental roles, and that the grandparents do not undermine this by keeping them in their child roles. In essence, structural family therapy focuses on changing a system through changing the structures of the system. For example, in a session, if a married couple are sitting apart, they may be asked to move their seating positions to sit next to each other before announcing to their children new boundaries they have decided upon. In this way, parental strength and unity are enacted in the present. Healthy families are considered to be those that can be flexible to social changes and that self-regulate and adapt to life-cycle developments, such as the transition from childhood to teenage years and leaving home.

> Family therapy uses techniques that alter the immediate context of people in such a way that their positions change. By changing the relationship between a person and the familiar context in which he functions, one changes his subjective experience. [Minuchin, 1974, p. 11]

This mirrors an organizational need to be adaptive to similar environmental and organizational life-cycle changes. Organizations that present as enmeshed become inward looking and self-obsessed and take their eye off their primary task and the external world. Within disengaged organizations, on the other hand, departments form rigid boundaries around functions, departments, and professions. They can lack a healthy culture of open communication, losing the emotional glue that binds an organization together, thus preventing what Senge called the "learning organization" (Senge, 1990). Structural family therapy offers a conceptual model that can be translated to organizational systems and, more importantly, offers managers, facilitators, and consultants well-researched and practised interventions that can be translated to work systems.

I am in favour of this systemic model because it engages with structural and spatial elements and also offers an account of power and authority, which is lacking in many systems approaches. Space, connectivity, structure, and power are elements that underpin much of my work as an organizational consultant.

A historical systemic perspective on the Quakers' use of dispersed leadership and emergent strategy

Historical perspectives are lacking in management literature (Burrell, 1997), and yet they illuminate organizational behaviour in new ways (Case & Gosling, 2007). I was influenced in this consultancy work by my PhD research, which focused on the Quaker egalitarian movement that had survived for over 350 years without formal and hierarchical leadership but utilized informal and dispersed leadership, based on a model of spiritual consensus. The longitudinal study of the Quakers showed how specific organizational spaces that emerged at their conception were institutionalized in their organizational structure, enabling emergent strategy and dispersed leadership to thrive.

The description in Box 8.1 outlines some of the important aspects of Quaker history relevant to this work (for further reading see Dandelion, 2007; Gwyn, 1984; Western, 2005).

My research identified how the Quakers had negotiated social change and survived over a 300-year period despite widespread persecution when most of the egalitarian and utopian social movements of the mid-seventeenth century disappeared. My findings were that the Quakers had survived not through visionary transformational leadership, which was apparent at the outset then faded in the second generation, but through the containing organizational structures and form of their worship and business meetings.

Box 8.1
Quaker organization

The Quakers' focus is on spiritual experience rather than on outward liturgy, church rituals, or trusting biblical "truth" as other puritans of their time did:

They believed the Bible had to be tested against the "truth within"; that the scriptures came secondary to one's own experience of the light. [Western, 2005, p. 337]

The Quakers' testimonies (core values) are Simplicity, Equality, Pacifism, and Truth.

Believing in a "priesthood of all believers" they (Quakers) were against the "hireling priests" of the established church believing its rituals such as baptism and communion were outward rituals of the world and it was the inner communion with Christ and the inner baptism of the spirit which really mattered. [Western, 2005, p. 338]

This meant that there was no appointed priesthood or official church hierarchy but that all members were able to take up the role of priest. This is often described as a leaderless organization, whereas the reality is that the Quakers are an early example of a "leaderful" (Starhawk, 1986) movement, encouraging a radical democratizing of leadership. In the 1650s they were social radicals who challenged privilege and power, especially the dominant powerful church, social standing, and gender. They enacted the "New Jerusalem" they sought in the form and structures of their new social movement and through their identity. They dressed in plain clothes, refused to doff their hats to those of higher social orders, refused to swear oaths in courts (as they claimed that truthfulness was part of everyday life, not something to be done on special occasions). Women broke gender roles and preached at open meeting and were activists throughout the organization (this was unheard of at the time even among radicals such as the Levellers). Margaret Fell, a prominent Quaker, wrote this public pamphlet in the late seventeenth century:

Those that speak against the power of the Lord speaking in a woman, simply by reason of her sex, or because she is a woman, not regarding the spirit ... such speak against Christ. [Trevett, 1995, p. 57]

(continued)

Each time a Quaker walked the street, went to court, or entered a church, they signposted an inversion of, and a confrontational challenge to, society's social norms and conventions that supported the existing power structures (Western, 2005).

The Quakers also refused to have a creed (or statement) of belief, which meant that theirs is a faith that is under constant review and is tested against the experience of the individual and discerned against the group. This creates a dynamic relationship between Quaker values and tradition and contemporary social norms. The truth becomes generative and narrative, paradoxically constrained by tradition and conservatism, but liberated by a lack of written creedal beliefs, which forced each generation to work on what "the truth" meant for their organization and for society as a whole. The Quakers provided an early and unusually sustainable example of dispersed leadership: decisions were (and are) made at their business meetings through spiritual consensus rather than by voting or through an elected leadership body.

It was the "paternal structure" of the organization, or its form, that provided the reflective "maternal spaces" necessary that enabled emergent strategy to arise from within the ranks of the organization and thus enabled adaptation to social change (Western, 2007). This liminal and counter-cultural space created by Quaker meetings for worship is formally structured, with minimal distractions. Instead of music, ritual, or spoken liturgy, there is silence and listening to the inner self and to the group. This is an egalitarian space, open to anyone present to "minister" (stand and speak) if "moved by the spirit" to do so. What is created is a space for reflection, for ideas and thoughts to emerge, as well as group discernment at business meetings using similar structures. This echoes with what Keats called "negative capability": the capacity to think and reflect without grasping for immediate solutions:

when a man is capable of being in uncertainties, Mysteries, doubts, without any irritable reaching after fact & reason. [Keats, 1817/1970, p. 43]

At times of crisis for their organization and during social change, local meetings for worship acted as "containers for anxiety" and places for "negative capability". This enabled the Quakers to change corporate direction and adapt to social change or, conversely, to get society to adapt to their discerned "truths". For example, the Quakers banned slavery in their own community 100 years prior to Wilberforce's campaign and were activists throughout this period to ban slavery in general.

In my consultancy practice, I use the concepts of paternal and maternal containment, which are psychoanalytic terms linked to human development (drawing on Bion, 1962; Klein, 1959; Lacan, seminar of 15 January, 1958, cited in Dor, 1977; Western, 2008). "Paternal containment" refers to structure, to form, to the external, and to what Freud called the reality principle. A good structure creates a secure container, which is a prerequisite for thinking, creativity, risk, and play.

"Maternal containment" is the unconscious emotional state that allows an infant to feel secure, play, think, and make sense of its own experience and to learn. I use these terms to describe how organizational spaces/structures create conscious and unconscious group processes that enhance or diminish learning and creativity. A huge influence in the consulting project has been the understanding of how containing spaces in organizations enable emergent strategy and dispersed leadership to be enacted.

Case study: Democratizing strategy

Background

This intervention emerged from my coaching relationship with the chief executive (CEO) of the Centre for Excellence in Leadership (CEL), an organization that was established to deliver leadership excellence in the further education and learning and skills sector in the United Kingdom. CEL was set up as a partner-based organization with three key players: two were university business and management schools, the other a public sector body from the learning and skills sector. The remit was to raise standards by delivering leadership development supported by research. This partner-based relationship was problematic from the outset, as are many partnership and collaborative enterprises, due to challenging contracting issues that created tensions over resources, clarity of roles, and diverse organizational cultures coming together. After working from one of the provider organizations in the first year and witnessing some of the challenges, I was asked by the CEO from CEL to become her personal leadership coach. The aims of this coaching relationship were initially to act as a sounding board and thinking partner to help her lead this new, ill-defined, and complex organization.

In the early coaching sessions with the CEO, we spent time drawing network maps of the system and the relationships, as well as personal maps of how she saw herself in the organization. We worked hard and fast, bouncing ideas around, and discussing how her leadership style and assumptions needed to adapt to lead this new organizational structure. She described her leadership style, which had been successful thus far leading further education colleges, as a dynamo-type leader, a catalyst for the organization at the centre of everything. She realized that to lead a partnership organization was a new challenge. Rather than being a dynamo at the centre, what was required was a new leadership approach that enabled leadership to be distributed throughout the organization. We worked on personal depth issues, how she managed her leadership role, and the projections from others. In parallel we worked on the strategic and structural issues of the system. We agreed that the leadership task was to create the structures and culture to allow CEL as an organization develop itself through entrepreneurial activity and to deliver at local levels while having a collective identity and common processes and branding. After coming up with "a picture" that represented the organizational architecture that could deliver some of the desired structural changes, the CEO then began to implement them.

We then turned our efforts to think about the organizational culture, and we agreed with Heifetz and Laurie (1997) that talent existed within the organization but the culture and structures needed to emancipate it:

Organizations rarely lack talented individuals, but they do frequently fail to bring those talents together to create a powerful collective force. In part this is due to the old-fashioned thinking that progress is only made when we have a "leader with vision" who can show us the way. This persistent image damages the collective capacity to do better things. [Heifetz & Laurie, 1997, p. 126]

Strategic forums

It was at this stage, as we looked at innovative ways to change the organizational culture, that we discussed and drew upon my PhD research on leadership and the Quaker movement. The CEO and I decided to try learn from and simulate aspects of the Quaker success in CEL. Our aim was to create spaces in the organizational architecture, or paternal containment, that would provide structures to open up a "maternal space" for creativity, emergent strategy and dispersed leadership. I was given the opportunity to move beyond my role as coach, while also maintaining it, to design and facilitate the delivery of this process.

This intervention had two key aims:

1. to democratize strategy by creating a radically inclusive strategic process that, as a by-product, would create opportunities for more distributed leadership;
2. to create an organizational form that allowed creativity, communication, and emergent ideas to flow from all parts of the organization.

We started with a modest idea to invite project leaders to participate in an open but structured process that we called a Strategic Forum. The idea was to engage a wider group than the CEO and senior management team to think strategically and take leadership initiatives.

Stage 1:
Project Leaders' Strategic Forum

The first Strategic Forum was held for those who led projects throughout CEL. We were explicit about our aim:

> *To democratize the strategic process by providing containing spaces within the organizational architecture to enable networking, open communication, and creativity to flourish.*

The Strategic Forum was structured and facilitated to:

» resist the rush to premature closure, avoiding problem-solving approaches
» free the participants from the responsibility of coming up with strategic plans
» avoid generating impotence and becoming stuck in the boggy lowlands of "negative thinking", while at the same time encouraging "truthful engagement".

To achieve this, the forum had a design that attempted to mirror the outcomes desired:

1. Space to (non)think.
2. Space to connect, to communicate, and to network.
3. Space to be creative.
4. Activities that "unbalanced" and deconstructed normative responses.

My role as facilitator closely mirrored the role of a structural family therapist: to join the system, as a "distant relative". I was known to many in the organization, but not part of it; I would be a part of the system, but distant enough to ask the difficult and naïve questions. The CEO attended at the beginning of the forum to legitimize it but did not attend through the event, as we thought this would free people up.

After an evening of "joining" in which the group came together, we then moved into a "free-association matrix" (Lawrence, 2000; Western, 2008). This exercise creates a space in which chairs are set out in an ad hoc jumbled fashion and participants are encouraged to sit in silence and then to "free-associate" their thoughts and preoccupations. This has the impact of "denaturalizing" a space, so that it becomes possible to "look awry" at the organization and to tap into the unconscious. It has some similar qualities to the Quaker meeting. To give a flavour of the free associations spoken in this session, a few examples are presented in Box 8.2. As you will see, this exercise releases ad hoc ideas that are later worked upon.

Box 8.2
Individuals speaking in the free-association matrix

"CEL is a honeycomb that needs to be full of honey—it has infrastructure already, so people will come to it."

"Don't be what others expect us to be."

"Create a sense of identity—we lost ours when we joined CEL."
"Identity relies on expertise."
"Create identity that we can live with—this is very hard, as we are all from different seconded organizations with strong identities of their own."

"Be aware of what we don't know."
"Don't be afraid of being experts." "What is our expertise?"
"Promote our learning . . ."
"Unlearning is most important."

"We should be called the Centre for unlearning leadership."
"Call ourselves Centre for Energy in Leadership."

"Is there a paradox between knowing and not-knowing?"
"CEL can say it's alright not to know."
"Blend vision, commitment, heart."

We followed the free associations with a small-group peer consultancy exercise to work on the themes that had emerged from the free associations, one of which was the identity of the whole organization.

The small-group conversations shifted the atmosphere dramatically. We had reached the emotional underbelly of how people had experienced the early months of this new organization. Trust had been built, and individuals were prepared to share their feelings. There was a feeling that mistakes had been made. People described feeling a sense of loss, as they were separated from their seconded institutions, and yet, in their new organization, they felt a little out of control. The partnerships were tense, often distrustful, and individuals working on the front line felt the pain of this acutely. The way the new organization had been structured meant that the internal partners were competing over resources, with little to reward collaboration. Senior leaders acknowledged this pain, and this released a lot of pent-up angst.

Powerful bonding was produced through the acknowledgement of mistakes, of painful relationships, and of how they had all tenaciously stuck at the difficult task to survive and produce successful results, in spite of the difficulties. CEL was only in its first year and the focus had been on survival, but now they could begin to build an improved culture. This led to a useful final session in the forum, in which questions of identity, community, and creating a culture where communication and risk taking and having the agency to act were strongly featured (Box 8.3).

The first emergent strategic decision from this forum was to decide, with the support of the CEO, that the Strategic Forums were so important that they should be made available to all staff. This was quite unexpected and exceeded our expectations. It was an enactment or bringing to life of the organization form we had discussed while planning the Strategic Forums. The thinking was that this forum and "space to think" was not just useful in itself, but would be an essential part of building a strong networked culture, and it would encourage improved communication across the organizational boundaries and help manifest the dispersed leadership we were attempting to achieve.

Box 8.3
Discussion points at the plenary
of the Project Leaders' Strategic Forum

Alignment

- *How do we go from "us and them" to "us and us"?*

- *Sense of purpose/belonging/ownership*

- *Community of communities*

- *Collective identity*

- *How are we a strategic force?*

- *How do we ensure operational delivery?*

What are the catalysts for change?

Permission: Taking our own authority and acting on it

Quality improvement, Confidence, Relationships

Skills development, No-blame culture (learn from failures)

Competence, Capability, Moving out of comfort zones

Final reflections

"Group felt like a breakthrough—very energetic, articulate."

"If we can be the catalyst for this, there will be the dawning of a new era."

"Maybe we have missed basic things; we need to go back to core basics and review where we failed—Be humble."

"More joining up can be done to fit a strategic picture."

"How do we manage the vast knowledge we have got?"

"Today has generated so much, there is not enough cross-fertilization."

"To be strategic will involve everyone."

Stage 2:
Radical inclusion

We invited four staff groups to attend the Strategic Forums in job-specific groups: Programme Delivery, Project Leaders, Central & Support staff, and Research & Evaluation. Three of these groups attended, while the fourth group, Research & Evaluation, was undergoing huge changes and facing deadlines before its contractual time with CEL was coming to an end. This meant that we did not manage to get this fragmented "group" to attend.

I designed each of the three Strategic Forums differently but with the same aims and basic structure. Again the CEO was present at the end of each one.

1. The first task of the strategy forum was cross-fertilizing information.

2. The second task was to create a new space from which open communication and new thinking could occur.

3. The third task was for the forum to offer content—some ideas that would contribute to the emerging strategy.

We made it clear that the work was not to create a strategic plan but to provide the groundwork for new strategies to emerge—that is, using "negative capability".

The structure of each forum was an evening and a day with space for reflection, communication, and cross-fertilization of ideas. We tried to encourage the idea that, whatever role individuals and teams played, their contribution was valuable and their ideas could make a difference that mattered. Box 8.4 shows two examples of systemic activities I used to promote this thinking.

The overall structure of the Strategic Forums, as well as these activities, were aimed at engaging individuals and teams to reflect on the interconnected nature of the workplace, the potential for improved communication, and the impact on the wider system of sharing information and making changes in one part of it. Individuals and groups shared practical ideas on how to improve operational performance, and strategic initiatives were widely supported, such as moving forward with an intranet to manage communication across CEL.

Box 8.4.
Systemic activities

Systems Game

This game is to demonstrate systemic and self-organizing/regulating principles. Two members of the group stand outside as the instructions are given to the rest of the group in a large, empty room.

Instructions:

- *Choose two people in the room without them knowing you have done so.*
- *When the game begins each person moves and keeps moving to create an equidistance of space between themselves and the two chosen others (this is not in-between the two people but triangulated with equal distance between all three of you).*

When the movement begins, the two outsiders come in and observe what is happening and are asked to describe (at the end of the exercise) what they see and think is happening.

The game continues for approximately 10 minutes.

What is created is a self-regulating system where small changes amplify, creating bigger changes. The movement slows and speeds up with its own momentum, and patterns emerge from what initially feels chaotic.

As one participant who held an administrative role said afterwards:

"This game showed me that even I can make a difference; it really hit me that we are all part of something but all rely on each other."

Another offered:

"It is really strange how we all slowed down but didn't stop, then I moved a bit faster and everyone moved; I felt powerful!"

We summarized this exercise thus:

- *shift the focus from self to focus on relationships*
- *there are self-organizing/regulating principles*
- *external influences force adaptive behaviour by organizations*
- *what looks like chaos is not always chaos; there can be self-managing systems in place*
- *constant change is needed to maintain stability*

(continued)

- *just because you don't know or understand, doesn't mean it isn't working*
- *every action has a reaction*
- *small things do make a change in the system*
- *CEL is a self-regulating mechanism: to stay the same (equilibrium) an organization has to be in a constant state of flux/change.*

Network Mapping

This exercise is based on the structural family therapy technique (Minuchin, 1974), which I have adapted and used with great success in organizations.

People using flip charts draw organizational maps using the symbols below to show how they (and their department/team) relate to other individuals and social groups—for example "the board", the "finance department", or even an abstract group such as "the customers" or a government agency.

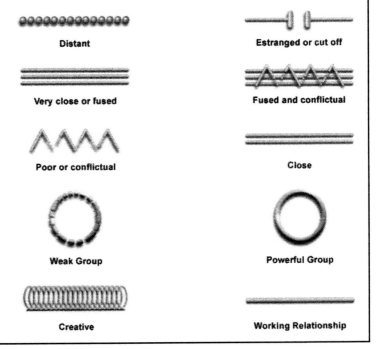

Distant	**Estranged or cut off**
Very close or fused	**Fused and conflictual**
Poor or conflictual	**Close**
Weak Group	**Powerful Group**
Creative	**Working Relationship**

At the centre of these maps I ask individuals to make a Plasticine effigy that symbolizes themselves. They then partner up and coach each other on their drawn networks, and the effigy can be moved to different parts of the system to look at the map and see the system from others' perspectives.

The maps are then put onto the walls, and people can walk around the gallery. A number of views and artistic impressions of the system emerge. Power and communication are key themes that arise from this activity.

Some comments that were made were:

Heightened awareness of relationships:

"Good to understand how relationships work."

"Perception of relationship is important."

"Closest you work with is where most of the conflict and creativity arises."

"Two people in the same office have different maps: the lesson is not to assume everyone sees world as we do."

Structural issues:

"No senior managers appeared on some maps, suggesting a distance and lack of direction from above?"

"Interestingly, 70% of delivery is done by external consultants, and yet they do not appear on the maps!"

"Maps say something about individuals and also about the organization."

"Not clear what each other's roles are—expand on job title to make it clear what everyone does."

Communications:

"Communications improving."

"Location less of an issue than it used to be, although visiting other sites still important."

Stage 3:
The whole system

When working as a family therapist, I realized the power of the extended family meeting. This physical face-to-face meeting, called to discuss some painful issues, somehow created a "witnessing" and acknowledgment of the issues and of the family bond that went beyond words. The Quakers, too, have an annual general meeting when the whole comes together; it is a powerful experience, with up to 1,000 Quakers making policy decisions through spiritual consensus.

The Strategic Forum design was to hold three separate forums and then bring these together at the annual staff day or dialogue, replicating the whole system, and which the CEO attended throughout.

Figure 7.1 illustrates how the Strategic Forums took place in different groups and then met as a whole system once a year (the Research & Evaluation forum did not take place).

As organizations grow and the boundaries blur as to where the organization starts and ends, it becomes important to find virtual ways to affirm collective identity. At the Annual Dialogue, each group was keen to share some of their experience. One group, led by a couple of dissatisfied staff, slipped into blame culture, but the whole group managed this in a mature way. A discussion on respect followed, and it was acknowledged that a culture of

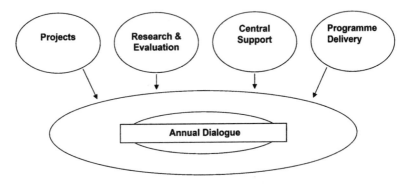

Figure 7.1.   The Strategic Forum design

respect needed nurturing, as the administration staff, in particular, felt that communications—e-mail and verbal—at times lacked respect. The sense of a more empowered group was in the room. We again did the Systems Game, enacting once more for the whole group how they are all connected and interdependent in a fun way.

Assessment

Our aim with this intervention was to introduce into CEL a form and structure that acted as both a signifier and a conduit of change. It simultaneously provided *physical spaces* that would encourage openness and creativity as well as distributing leadership. Employees could engage and partake in strategic thinking and, in doing this, could subvert a hierarchical and dependent culture that was getting in the way of change and collaboration.

From a systemic perspective, this idea works on the premise that leadership is not the property of a single individual, or a hierarchical concept, but exists within an organizational and social ecology (see "Eco-leadership", in Western, 2008). I was also bringing psychoanalytic theory together with my family systems background. In approaching this work in the way that I did. I drew on the theory of paternal and maternal containers to create spaces in the organizational architecture, thereby structurally changing the system in order to stimulate further change. I learned from the Quakers' experience of creating such spaces and allowing/trusting in dispersed leadership and emergent strategy, rather than feeling under pressure to conform to social norms and become another hierarchical organization. My experience of structural family therapy helped me to acknowledge and consider power relations in the attempt to encourage distributed leadership, as this will not work if the issue of power is ignored. It was important to bring the CEO to these forums at the beginning or the end—not to dominate the meetings, but to legitimize them and engage openly and frankly in discussion. At the Annual Dialogue, the CEO made an honest and soul-bearing comment on feedback she had received about her leadership style, and how she, like others, was working hard to make changes in order to further change the organizational culture. This was "signifying leadership" at its best and brought power into the open so that it was available for debate and negotiation.

I have identified three key themes that were highlighted as benefits at the Annual Dialogue:

» *Distributed leadership*

This went beyond rhetoric, as change initiatives were suggested from all parts of the organization, some of the best coming from administrative staff. Together these form an emergent strategy, particularly in relation to improving processes and communication and sustaining social networks.

» *Identifying what is sustainable success: short- and long-term goals*

There was a shift from the struggle for survival and reactive management to being able to consider a strategic future. This was the biggest success produced by the intervention.

» *Designing and adapting business models that work for the whole of CEL*

Structural and process decisions were made that addressed CEL as a whole rather than as individual parts. It was very rewarding for me to watch people think and talk in their own language about the whole system and connectivity.

CEL has been very successful as an organization and has overachieved its delivery targets, as well as becoming a much less frenetic and fragmented place. It was evaluated as follows:

> By 31 March 2007, less than four years after its launch, the Centre for Excellence in Leadership (CEL) had recruited nearly 26,000 individual participants and worked with 91 per cent of the organisations in the further education system. CEL's annual review, published today, also shows that 12,000 participants were recruited during the financial year to 31 March 2007, exceeding the target by 46 per cent, and that customer satisfaction had improved again, with 96 per cent of participants rating CEL's programmes, courses or events as good or very good.
> [retrieved July 13, 2007, from www.centreforexcellence.org.uk]

Internal communication has improved through the implementation of an intranet and staff bulletins. Leadership has been distributed—for example, groups of self-appointed staff now organize the annual away-days, which are popular and fun. There are also improved systems of internal appraisal, with a new incentive scheme for all staff. Structurally there have been major changes, with newly appointed directors further dispersing leadership from central control to those closer to delivery.

The process of democratizing strategy has supported this success and has been one of many factors rather than the sole causal factor.

Conclusions and discussion

It is always a challenge to persuade senior management in an organization to commit to a process like this in a world of controlling costs and functionalist thinking. This is because:

1. It is counter-cultural and threatening to be part of a process to change the culture so as to disperse leadership and power. It is important that consultants working with this kind of intervention can contain the anxiety of leaders.

2. If such a systemic intervention is to work, it is very important to persuade HR teams and senior managers to address power issues. While problematic, it is not impossible if the gains of a more transparent, communicative engaged, and innovative culture can be argued for.

3. It is a skilful business to manage and facilitate these forums. They can easily become sites of blame culture, particularly if the participants feel that the work is nothing but management rhetoric. Cynicism has grown since a raft of transformational leadership initiatives between the 1980s and 2000 were trumpeted with prophetic fervour yet failed to deliver. This is why the power relations in such an intervention, as well as improved dialogue, need to be addressed.

Management thinking is usually done "ahistorically", as if the data from the contemporary era is all we have to go on. The example of a longitudinal case study of the Quakers and their use of distributed leadership and system adaptation over 350 years has inspired my own work. I would encourage other consultants and leaders to explore the history of systems and movements as opposed to a history of individual hero leaders.

4.   Finally, it is my belief that a key leadership task is to liberate strategy and totalizing power from the manacles of the boardroom. This is because we are now in a context where most organizations, not just CEL, will not survive without effective partnership working and ways of motivating and inspiring staff by including them in decision-making. Leaders will need to create a reflexive system enabling strategy to be aligned with an organizational culture that maximizes participation. It will increasingly be the task of systemic consultants and managers to find ways to support others to help make this happen.

CHAPTER NINE

Coaching lawyers to lead

Georgina Noakes & Myrna Gower

Commentary

In the third of the three chapters on leadership development, Georgina Noakes & Myrna Gower write about the leadership programme they developed for partners at a London law firm. The interest in this work is how it arose out of a systemic analysis of the organization-development needs of the law firm, sparked off by research undertaken by the consultants into what legal assistants wanted from partners.

In order to remain competitive, partners needed to be more effective leaders and to move from seeing themselves as "lone practitioners to collaborative co-owners". This required them to develop their internal and external communication and business development skills. The vehicle for organizational development was thus a form of teaching and learning for individual lawyers that was very much in keeping with the pre-existing individualistic culture of a partnership business, but would result in a more collaborative working environment.

A great deal of care was taken over the design of the programme so that it kept a strong business focus and supported the lawyers in applying their skills in the work situation over a period of time. For example, the four modules were called "Managing Myself", "Managing Others", "Managing Clients", and "Managing Profitability". There were monthly workshops, reading assignments, tasks set between workshops, as well as individual coaching. Noakes & Gower created tailor-made activities and exercises designed to help participants develop increased confidence in offering feedback and in leading and coaching others.

Bearing in mind the ambivalence towards the programme in the law firm and the possibility that it could get "killed off", they paid careful attention to devising ways to collect participant feedback and hold regular meetings with the leaders in the wider firm so they could ensure it was fully supported and relevant. They appreciated all they needed to do to contain the anxiety and huge philosophical shift in global view the partners needed to make.

The value of this chapter for the reader considering development of a leadership or other training programme within an organization is to be able to see it, as Noakes & Gower did, as an organizational intervention. This meant that they needed to be able to think and work with the whole system at every stage in the process even if they were only actually "teaching" 12 of them at a time. They were particularly adept at keeping close enough to the existing culture to be acceptable, but different enough to bring about quite an ambitious change.   [Eds.]

This chapter is about how two consultants developed a Partner Leadership & Coaching Programme over four years at a City of London law firm. The programme grew out of research undertaken at the firm by the consultants and took two years' to negotiate and construct. The consultants were commissioned to run three programmes, each of which took a year to deliver.

Coaching and key systemic considerations
that informed our work

Historically, coaching has been keen to stress that it is not therapy (Hart, Blattner, & Leipsic, 2001; Kilburg, 2002; Peltier, 2001). Initially, coaching in business was goal-orientated, short-term, and concerned with achieving the highest possible performance. One of the original coaching models—Whitmore's (1992) "GROW" sequence of questioning, **G**oal, **R**ealities, **O**ptions, **W**ill—was designed to generate "prompt action and peak performance". As the coaching community has prospered and its body of knowledge widened, it has expanded to include the interest and participation of professionals from the psychological arena. This has led to the start of collaborative ventures typified by this project.

The ten concepts listed below created the core knowledge base of the programme. The goal was to create a common language as we built a "community of understanding" (Gergen, 1994) within each Partner Leadership & Coaching group.

1. first- and second-order change;

2. understanding behaviour in the context of the wider system;

3. shifting from linear to circular thinking;

4. seeing and understanding patterns that connect;

5. studying feedback loops;

6. exploring ideas of resistance to change;

7. questioning techniques;

8. use of narrative;

9. brief-solution ideas;

10. appreciative inquiry.

We will return to develop these ideas but first want to describe the context for coaching in the legal sector. We then describe how we positioned ourselves to be invited to run the leadership and coaching programmes and how we co-created the composition of the programme with leaders at the firm. We then describe how the programmes were delivered.

The context for coaching—how the legal landscape has changed over the last twenty years— and why leadership is now significant for lawyers

In common with any other market, there is a finite pool of business available to the legal profession. Especially during economic downturns, and because of increased competition between firms, the recruiting of new clients, retention of existing business, and maintenance and development of good staff should be the mainstays of professional practices.

With this in mind, law firms have begun to go beyond the "letter of the law". A focus on relationship management has developed, both externally with clients and prospects and internally with legal and professional services staff, to enhance their profitability.

Unlike a corporate structure, in a legal partnership each partner, especially an equity partner, is an owner investor or a future owner investor in the business. Partners' integrity and influence are underpinned by the fees they generate, for themselves or their teams. If their billing rate does not significantly contribute to profits (after overheads and salaries are paid), invariably their partnership status is at risk and their membership of the firm will be challenged.

Lawyers, by dint of their profession, are intelligent, articulate, and ambitious. Their legal expertise, however, does not necessarily translate into management, leadership, or team-building skills. The lawyers who are exceptional seem to know how to manage themselves. They manage the complex webs of relationships in which they operate—both internally and externally, with clients, influencers, and introducers of new work.

How do we, as executive coaches,
obtain new contracts?

Whether you are a consultant, an executive coach, or a lawyer, the steps required to engage in a new piece of business are as subtle and complex as any well-choreographed dance. Creating new business requires research, preparation, patience, and tenacity. It requires the courage to ask for, and then do, the work—all at a price that adds value to both you and to the organization.

The story begins in 1999. I (Georgina) was editing a magazine for lawyers run as a joint venture with a public relations (PR) company, who were already doing work at the City firm featured in this chapter. The PR company arranged an introductory lunch between myself and the legal firm's new director of HR.

The director of HR and I met regularly over the next year or so, sharing our ideas and philosophy about how to use coaching to develop the communication and business development skills of lawyers at the firm.

The HR director decided to commission a piece of research from my company on what the senior legal staff, the assistants, thought about working at this firm.

The key themes were that assistants wanted more feedback from partners; they wanted to know what they were meant to be doing and how they fitted into the big picture of the legal transactions as well as the teams with which they were working. They did not want to wait until their annual appraisal to hear from partners how they were performing.

The managing partner at the time (who was later to become the senior partner) and one or two of the heads of department (one of whom was to take over as managing partner), along with the director of HR, felt it was important that there was some kind of course developed for partners to address the results of the assistants survey. It was recognized that leadership skills and a collaborative, coaching style would need to be developed, and it was out of this context and story that the Partner Leadership & Coaching programme was constructed and negotiated.

It was to be the largest investment the firm had made to date on developing the non-legal skills of its partners and was to put this firm in a position of being a pioneer in the legal marketplace when it came to its commitment to developing the leadership, communication, and coaching skills of partners on a long-term, rather than short-term, basis.

It was clear that such a programme would require two executive coaches. We (Georgina & Myrna) had already been working together at another professional services firm in the City. After meeting with the managing partner and the HR director, it was agreed that we should both work on this project. The firm liked the idea of mixing commercial and coaching experience, on the one hand (GN), with systemic, academic, and clinical expertise, alongside many years' experience of working with leaders in organizational life, on the other (MG).

Co-creating the composition of the programme

We had to decide what principles would inform our input. How would we design the input, and what would be incorporated in the content? How would we sell these ideas to lawyers?

We had to take into account that we would be working with experts in their respective fields. They had years of training in how to interview, to inquire, to investigate. The *raison d'être* of their work is to develop argument and to proffer expert advice.

The recognition of two factors stopped us in our tracks when we realized they could give us an entry point and a foundation from which to enter their world. First, we were acutely aware that lawyers are accustomed to adopting different interpretations of the law, whether in contentious or non-contentious practice. Second, we also knew that the regular meetings they held with their clients were core to them developing coherent understandings of a client brief. We realized that they were building narratives, a process to which we could add.

We believed that using a systemic approach to the thinking and design of the programme could help lawyers understand more about the complex web of relationships that surrounded them. It would offer a theoretical framework and help them recognize how to trigger change.

*The theoretical underpinnings
that shaped the programme delivery*

Prior to explaining the overall programme design and how participants were selected, we now return to the ten key ideas used to underpin the specific content of the programme.

First- and second-order change

We were interested in integrating Watzlawick's ideas of what he called "first-order" incremental change in organizational life and "second-order" change "where organizational paradigms, norms, ideologies or values are transformed in some fundamental ways" (Watzlawick, Weakland, & Fisch, 1974).

It was our hope to ensure some second-order change. We aimed to do this by working longer term with partners (over a one-year period), where they could share learning and observe themselves and their peers in the context of a group dynamic and then return to work to "practise while they performed" (Bennis & Thomas, 2002) their role as lawyers.

In addition to monthly group workshops, monthly one-to-one coaching conversations were designed to reflect on the group process: learning that had taken place when they practised systemic ideas in the context of their legal teams and client work. The personal coaching would also celebrate small successes and would focus on continued personal challenges in adopting new paradigms, norms, ideologies, and values. The monthly coaching conversations were where we were most likely to observe first hand, over time, any fundamental second-order transformation taking place.

Understanding behaviour
in the context of the wider system

We wanted to take the spotlight off the individual lawyer. We hoped to help them adopt a "balcony position" (Bennis & Thomas, 2002) where our lawyers would be encouraged to observe the whole "stage" of relationships that surrounded them, as well as to understand more about the cast of the characters that made up their law firm and marketplace.

Our goal was to help partners to shift from seeing behaviour as an individual "quirk" to understanding their own behaviour—as well as that of their colleagues and clients—in the context of family and organizational dynamics.

We connected lawyers' leadership stories to the narratives learned from their family stories.

Shifting from linear to circular thinking

Adopting a systemic position towards organizational life required a shift of mind to see the world anew (Senge, 1990).

This involved coaching our lawyers to shift their thinking from cause and effect (blame) to feedback loops and circularity—from what Haslebo and Nielsen (2000) explain as a shift from "the linear to the circular line of thinking".

The linear approach locks individuals in patterns where they do not see themselves in relation to others nor to the wider system. It encourages a culture of blame, and this is a paradigm in which an organization is often stuck when a coach is called in. The language of blame is commonly used in legal practices.

Seeing and understanding patterns that connect

In the circular approach, say Haslebo and Nielsen (2000), fragments and segments are assembled into a larger whole and the attention is shifted away from individuals to the circular pattern of relationships, thoughts, and actions: "when the idea of cause is taken out of the equation, so is blame" (p. 104).

Curiosity takes the place of condemnation—so instead of finding the guilty parties (something litigation lawyers are trained, and love, to do), it becomes much more relevant to uncover the part that each person played in creating and maintaining the pattern of events and actions. But Haslebo and Nielsen also stress the importance of each individual taking responsibility for his or her own actions and dialogue within the system, an idea that we echoed in the one-to-one coaching conversations.

The examination of a pattern is based on the assumption that everyone is, to some extent, responsible for its existence and, therefore, for changing it. A pattern can be changed at any time by any person who, through altering their own behaviour or asking a question, can introduce *difference* (Bateson, 1972, p. 381).

Studying feedback loops

To help shift partners from seeing themselves as lone practitioners to collaborative co-owners, we concentrated on exploring the systemic idea of feedback loops. O'Neill (2000), using ideas from family therapy, calls them "social interactional fields" (p. 43). We adopted her metaphor of a spider's web.

Our purpose was to help our lawyers identify the feedback loops of which they were a part and to see themselves "as a web of forces, some for and some against change" (Campbell, 1995, p. 22).

The firm's appraisal system provided us with a golden opportunity to describe feedback loops. The appraisal system offered a practice ground for partners to experiment with their own capacity to observe and to offer feedback, not just on an annual basis but to become confident enough to give feedback on a day-to-day basis. To this end we introduced the reflecting conversation (Andersen, 1987), where we invited partners to begin to sharpen their observation skills in the group. This raised the level and quality of feedback from those partners, which enhanced their influence among their peers.

Exploring ideas of resistance to change

As a key concept of systemic thinking, we knew we would have to explore resistance to change. We asked our lawyers to observe in what ways a desire for the status quo was observable at partner meetings and to what lengths partners would go to maintain a *"balanced"* (Bateson, p. 437; emphasis in original) system.

Attempts to change the system or parts of it can be seen to encounter resistance, since it operates as an integrated whole and strives to maintain homeostasis (Jackson, 1957, p. 79). We encouraged our lawyers to work with resistance, rather than against it.

Questioning techniques

Commensurate with legal expertise, we took the idea of questioning and invited the partners to begin to demonstrate their well-established skills in this domain. We offered them different descriptions of questions to support their objectives, and for the first time they began to connect with the idea of inviting new information. This was contrary to most questioning where the lawyer may not be looking for new information but, rather, asking the client to confirm what is already known. Taking a position of curiosity was seen by the group to be "unscientific" and, without prepared theoretical positioning, may have been resisted outright.

Our lawyers found it difficult to open themselves to the unknown but were surprised when they took a risk or two. This usually occurred at a point of difficulty when all their usual skills had not brought results. One partner said: "*I have tried asking questions with a problem client, and it has worked*".

Use of narrative

Good legal advice stands upon reasoned descriptions, based on full and comprehensive detail.

We invited our lawyers, when they were being briefed by their clients, to ask questions they would not normally ask. This led them to hear new information that developed their narratives and often altered their approach to the matter at hand. We invited them to ascribe and articulate the meanings that they gave to what they heard from their clients. We talked about placing their own meanings in conjunction with the explanations offered by their clients. New stories unfolded as they identified narratives that had beginnings, middles, and endings. The closer collaboration with their clients resulted in their finding a different way of explaining to themselves how they made sense of events.

Epston (in Epston, White, & Murray, 1992) argues that the expression of our experience through stories shapes our performance. Through the extended interpretation of the brief, these lawyers began to note the impact on their advice and actions: *"I understand better the dynamics of client relationships (and surrounding issues) and achieve a better outcome."* Confidence and a new-found safety was reported as an outcome of this different emphasis in their collaboration with clients.

Brief-solution ideas

The partners on the programme responded to the immediacy of *brief-solution ideas* (De Shazer, 1985). They enjoyed the format it gave them for offering feedback and liked the instant strategies it gave them. They found they were able to put into immediate practice the formulaic questioning (from finding exceptions to expressing visions of a different future and agreeing the likelihood of a way forward). It gave us a structure for a conversation that became an important format to assist their coaching of others.

Through various exercises and tasks set, we gave partners an opportunity to rehearse their observational skills and learn to offer immediate feedback.

Brief-solution ideas posed a challenge to the presiding culture, which believed that the way forward was to learn from mistakes rather than from successes.

Appreciative inquiry

Lawyers are trained to be critical, and their judgement is deemed as a crucial part of their armoury. However, when translated into day-to-day development and motivation of their legal teams, these qualities did not seem to create a favourable climate for peak performance.

We introduced the notion of *appreciative inquiry* as a valuable tool to help them investigate what worked well in their teams, and with certain individuals, and to offer feedback based on what they had observed.

* * *

These ten systemic ideas were woven into the core of the programme design.

Programme design

The feedback indicated a need for a shift in partner behaviour that would lead to an increased confidence both in offering feedback to others and in leading and coaching them.

It was agreed that there were four key criteria for partners' performance. These were how they "managed themselves", "managed others", and "managed clients", and, last but by no means least, the role they took in "managing the profitability" of the firm to ensure sustainable growth and increased fees.

» Thus the programme consisted of four modules, one module for each of the four criteria identified above. Each module consisted of three workshops, which took place on a monthly basis, and each module took three months to complete. The overall programme (Modules 1–4) therefore took one year to complete.

» The workshops took place on a monthly basis. Bearing in mind that partners are charged out per hour, we were aware that this would be an expensive consideration and could conflict with general partner beliefs that this may not be a valuable use of their billable time.

» Reading assignments recommended included material selected from the firm's law library—*Legal Business* and *The Commercial Lawyer* magazines, *Legal Week*, *Harvard Business Review*—and a regular trawl of the legal pages from the press to inform debate. Several publications on leadership were included to encourage partners' personal narratives. Theoretical papers or chapters were carefully selected, focusing on coaching and systems theory. We had to watch out not to overwhelm the group with too much material that would not get read in between their managing a demanding client portfolio.

» Tasks were set between each workshop (examples given later).

» Each lawyer had monthly one-hour coaching conversations with both authors present to ensure individual integration and application of ideas covered in the workshops into their practice.

» The group participants completed feedback documents at the end of Modules 1 and 4 respectively.

Selection of participants

The aim was to invest in the existing talents of partners to ensure that they were given the ongoing support and skills needed as they continued their development at the firm. The criteria for choosing delegates was based primarily on candidates whom the director of HR had identified as potentially benefiting from the group and one-to-one learning experience that the programme was to offer. However, each candidate put forward already showed a broad spectrum of skills—ranging from the ability to consider and apply new ideas to a track record of finding creative solutions to difficult problems.

Each partner, after reading a briefing paper and attending an exploratory conversation with us both as the executive coaches, was given the option to attend or not. The 12 partners created a manageable group dynamic. Previous experience of group work and training had showed us that this number would give us the flexibility to develop a cohesive group, allowing for absences without losing the viability of the dialogue within it. It was also important that the group was large enough for there to be partners within it who would not normally come into contact or have the opportunity to collaborate, with one another. Finally, a group of 12 was easily divisible, so that we could complete the individual coaching over a two-day period, based on seeing six people a day. This made financial sense both to them and to us.

Specific programme content

Module 1: "Managing Myself"

In order to introduce partners to their personal contexts, we started with the paradigm *"Managing Myself"*. We wanted them to develop insight into "their whole" by understanding their links with others and how these interactions began to meld with the system of which they were a part. In the feedback after the closure of the programme, several participants reported that the development of their own personal genograms had presented startling discoveries.

Among other questions, they were asked to identify the factors that they thought contributed towards their choice to become lawyers. Reflecting on her genogram and the strong examples set by her maternal grandmother and by her mother, one partner said: *"I had no idea that I had leadership skills and what they were . . . this has been a major leap for me in at least recognizing that these skills exist."*

At the beginning of the programme, personal disclosure was not common practice. Such disclosures were viewed as being counter to the tightly held boundary between "the office" and "home". Partners usually made concerted efforts to keep personal matters away from the office.

Example Tasks:

From the drawing of their personal genograms, partners were encouraged to have a conversation with a family member about their leadership style and to seek out the family's view on how come they became a lawyer.

A Leadership Profile was completed, and partners were asked to observe specific behaviours identified in their practice.

Module 2: "Managing Others"

With some novel ideas about their personal profiles in hand, we moved on to explore the impact of this new knowledge when *"Managing Others"* within the firm.

We focused on developing partners' listening and feedback skills. We introduced circular questioning (Selvini Palazzoli, 1986) at this stage. They began to question their assumptions as they experimented with different ways to lead their teams: *"It helps to understand that people who on the face of it have similar goals actually have different ways of getting there. This recognition is very important to cohesive teamwork,"* reflected one partner.

By this stage, partners were beginning to recognize their own repeating patterns of interaction and wanted to look at those when with clients.

Example Tasks:

Partners were asked to identify three relational questions and interview a colleague using them.

Partners were asked to identify specific repeating patterns of behaviour in a partners meeting.

A supervised coaching task was given that involved each partner having to coach one assistant over a three-month period.

Module 3: "Managing Clients"

The programme had laid down some important theoretical ideas that had been practised with supervision. *"Managing Clients"* was a natural next step. We began to assist partners to identify their own personal marketing styles based on the kind of interactions that worked best for each of them—for example, better in larger groups or preferring more intimate communication. For example, having become more familiar with asking questions to test their assumptions, partners became more confident to enter into dialogue, saying: *"I have asked a client to talk about his business rather than my just 'selling' the firm to him, and he was delighted to tell me all about it"*; *"It has made me think in particular about having discussions with clients and asking open questions."*

They had begun to recognize the effect of their behaviours in a feedback loop. They cottoned on to the idea that consideration of their interactions within context offered them a different direction.

This led straight to fostering closer client relationships and even to getting new business: *"After several visits from my partner and me, to discuss the challenges this company was facing in terms of their legal work and to show our interest in them as people and as a business, we got our first instruction from them—and have had several more since".*

Example Tasks:

Partners were asked to develop their marketing profile. This was based upon new-found knowledge about themselves and their personal values and leadership style, and how these fitted into the wider context of the firm. For example, each partner was tasked with developing a personal business plan and then seeing how that dovetailed with the plan of the team or department in which they worked.

The group was asked to prepare a pitch presentation for new work based upon information provided on a current market/client issue— for example an M&S takeover bid undertaken by the Information & Research unit at the firm. This was an opportunity to apply theoretical ideas in practice and to receive feedback in turn from us and their colleagues. These sessions were filmed.

Module 4: "Managing profitability"

The final section of the programme was directed at *"Managing profitability"*. It was critical here to contextualize the position of "the bottom line". We explored partners' relationship to fee earning and its implications for their position in the firm. Ultimately partner performance is judged by the fees they generate, and how much money they contribute to "the profitability pot" after overheads and salaries are paid. Lawyers commonly, by reason of their integrity and professionalism, are reluctant to negotiate with clients about fees, and we made this area the context for this module (Hodgart & Mayson, 2006).

Once partners began to practise their negotiation skills, they found this had an immediate impact on the bottom line, which in turn raised their profile as a partner. One partner, able to use his new-found delegation and negotiation skills, recovered a fee on a transaction that represented enough money to pay for the

Partner Leadership & Coaching Programme that year. As this all fed back into the wider organization, the programme was affirmed as an important resource. When the topic of "profitability" was finally centralized and became part of the meaning system, the programme, with each partner treated as integral to it, began to receive acclaim.

Example Task:

As a means to becoming more profitable in their own practices, part-ners were encouraged to delegate work to assistants. Given that this process usually invites resistance, partners were asked in the first instance to identify potential work for delegation and, where appro-priate, to use the skills learned to put this into practice. Partners fed back on their activities in the large group and in their one-to-one meetings.

The philosophical standpoint that organized the thinking of these partners as they approached their work

When we interviewed the partners prior to the programme, it was not surprising to hear of their individualistic ideas about their positions in the firm. They saw themselves mainly as unidirec-tional in the advice they offered. Their perception was that clients came for advice and representation, and it was their duty to fulfil this instruction. They thought it was a lone task to climb the pro-fessional ladder and that being made a partner was acknowledge-ment and testament to this hard-earned routine. This pathway they saw to be inevitably filled with challenge and discomfort.

While most of the partners interviewed worked as part of a team, they reported that their billing levels were self-determined and believed that they each had now to "grow themselves" to a new level to validate their selection as partners. Being an "inde-pendent thinker" was commensurate with authority and gravitas. High fee earners were valued, even if their relational skills created conflict and dissatisfaction. The lawyers questioned respected the hierarchical arrangements of the firm, and their position in that order reflected where they thought that they stood in terms of their own career development. Profitability was the single most important organizing construct.

The general hypotheses guiding our programme brief

» In our planning, we envisaged that the programme would need to be designed as an intervention that would make a significant difference. The programme would encourage a philosophical shift from an individualistic and self-directing model to one that included context and feedback as working principles. The course content would offer some theoretical models of change to underpin its practical applications. We realized that this would be viewed as unusual and that the introduction of psychological or any other new language and concepts would have to be carefully approached to avoid rebuff.

» The title, "The Partner Leadership & Coaching Programme", would immediately redefine how partners saw themselves. They would be invited to participate as "Leaders"—a position they had not previously considered for themselves. Interactive and action-based learning would be encouraged by introducing live supervision of their own coaching of others.

» This philosophical shift would need to become observable at partner level as well as firm-wide.

» Regular feedback between programme leaders would be maintained with the wider firm. Meetings with the senior and managing partners, together with head of HR, were deemed essential if the programme was to ensure regular partner attendance and be successfully viewed by others in the firm as a good investment in their development. The Managing and Senior partners and head of HR would be invited to present to the programme participants.

» Above all, confidentiality would have to be seen to be absolute if there were to be any chance of partners experimenting with new ideas. Partners would have to be protected by us and be reassured that they would not at any time be compromised in the eyes of the firm. Their trust in us would have to be implicit. We realized that no mean task lay ahead.

First barriers that demanded early attention

Partners asked themselves, "what was the meaning of selection to go on to the programme for the partners?" and immediately thought that they had failed to achieve the firm's expectations and were being sent on the programme for remedial purposes. At the other end of the spectrum, some partners thought programme attendance would be a passport to becoming an equity partner. Implicit here was a belief that partners had no choice but to attend in order to keep, or develop, their position in the partnership.

We elected to spell out the qualities required for selection on the programme. We insisted that partners had the *choice* to participate, and although being recommended for the programme generated specific meanings for each partner, and caused some concerns, these were addressed over the course of the programme. There was considerable internal ambivalence and some vocal opposition to the investment required to run the programme. The firm had never before spent such a large amount of money on personal and professional development, nor had such large amounts of partner time been asked for.

We knew we had to pay meticulous attention to the context of the programme and its position in relation to the wider context of the firm. To this end a substantial briefing paper that included a comprehensive description and rationale of the programme was sent as a draft to them before being presented to the management board of the firm. This process helped to overcome the sceptical views of some partners as expressed in the management debate, so that the go-ahead to the programme was given.

The collaboration between ourselves and the HR director and the Senior and Managing partners remained ongoing, ensuring they all remained in the loop and were thus able to counter continuing pockets of resistance, especially during the first year of the programme. All were participant to the regular designing and delivery of the programme in line with the continuing feedback from the participating lawyers. It was important that they were always armed with sufficient material with which to justify and value the firm's investment in the programme.

Reflections on what we have learned: what do we think happened?

We viewed the firm as a whole organization comprised of functional units, each relating to the other. We saw the system situated not only in a wider community but also in response to it. The ongoing feedback loops developed their complexity as they responded to the constant to and fro of information.

What we attempted in the programme was to find a genuine position where we created a platform for an interdisciplinary view of knowledge that allowed for different subsets of knowledge to interact. In doing so, we believe that we developed new systems of understanding and communicating such that instead of us simply "teaching" ideas or communicating information, we evolved what Hoffman (1993) talks about as "actualized meaning".

It is very difficult to alter one's global view, and, in some respects, we had asked our group(s) to begin to view their worlds with different lenses, a fundamental basis for change. We were rigorous in our insistence that they show active application of ideas they might absorb, and we supported whatever they tried to do as generously as possible.

We reminded them that while they could not control their environment, they could, in Hoffman's (1993) words, "perturb it and see how it compensates". She would say (p. 21) that she gives the environment a bump and then watches it jump!

What could have been done differently?

Many elements of our programme were organized by our eagerness to ensure that we did not displease either the key proponents of the programme or the group participants. There was a lot of money at stake, and high expectations as a result. These tensions often organized meetings and inevitably affected group tasks. More frequent external supervision for us as the coaches could have addressed some of our concerns. This might have enabled us to be more flexible in the programme, making it possible to relinquish planned tasks in favour of group debate at certain times.

As the programmes progressed our sponsors in the firm seemed to see it less and less necessary to meet with us as the coaches. While this reflected the trust and confidence we had built between us all, in retrospect we, as the coaches, should have been more firm in negotiating the importance of regular reviews. This would have facilitated a more regular feedback loop between the coaches and the sponsors. It would have encouraged us, as well as connected the programme more fully into the wider firm.

Many elements of programme content—exercises and reading in particular—would be useful to review. We would add more to the content. We might alter exercises, become bolder with theoretical building blocks, build new ones, and pay novel attention to these ideas in relation to profitability.

The use of the one-to-one meetings with partners may well need less structure on some occasions and need to be more task-focused on others.

Perhaps our greatest omission was in failing to create a context for the programme to feed back to the wider partnership. This has been left to the key proponents of the programme and one or two partner participants. Our own practice needed to be more coherent with the ideas that we shared with the group. We needed to demonstrate ourselves and the group being in an ongoing dialogue with the wider partnership. This way, information about the outcomes of the programme could have become better integrated and more valued as part of the larger culture of the organization.

End word

We attempted to hold a fine balance and to create an environment of "safe uncertainty" (Mason, 1993), where partners could explore tensions between their personal and work situations. Bringing the personal self into the work environment is difficult for lawyers. It was necessary for us to supervise this practice carefully and invite acknowledgement around the smallest of changes. This sometimes created dilemmas, and it was vital to offer reassurance.

After a programme that spanned almost five years, with three different groups from the partnership, we felt it was important to make symbolic gestures at ending. HR and management said (as contracted) that all partners for whom they wanted this intervention had benefited for the moment. They now wished to move on to attending programmes for assistant lawyers. This would be a new venture.

At a celebratory lunch organized by the managing partner, we presented the partnership with a photographic print of a mountain (the Matterhorn), which we thought reflected their climb, their courage, the continuing challenge in the face of the unknown, and we inscribed it: "The Leading Edge."

This seemed to us to summarize the innovative approach the firm had taken in its willingness to take the risk of developing a Leadership & Coaching Programme that had made a difference not just to the participants but to the partnership as a whole.

Final thoughts

David Campbell & Clare Huffington

We began this book by discussing the strengths and weaknesses of the systemic model. The continual search for meaning that is part of systemic practice provides a way of generating different perspectives. These can release the organization and its members from being stuck in their thinking. And, at a certain point, they need to capture the meanings and use them as a basis for action. At this time, life becomes binary—will we or won't we decide this or that? It is perhaps in contrast with the relative comfort of the binary requirements of leadership and management that systemic thinking acquires its real value. And it may also make life more difficult, in that it may introduce more complexity and ambiguity into the system!

It has been interesting to reflect on why we thought of editing this book at this particular time. Why might we have wanted to highlight systemic approaches to organizational consultation when consultancy to the whole system is actually on the decline? At the same time, one-to-one and team developmental approaches are on the increase. There is something paradoxical about this: as organizational boundaries loosen and organizations need to become skilful at new tasks, such as partnership working and strategic alliances, it is somewhat counter-intuitive to find individuals in organizations seeking support for themselves rather than for the whole system. Some of the answers may lie in the experience of working with these individuals and teams in coaching relationships. They appear to be struggling with the failure of traditional hierarchical leadership in combination with managing the difficulties of lateral relationships—for example, in partnership working—as these come more into the foreground of organizational life (Huffington & Miller, 2008). It seems that they feel vulnerable and need a private space to work out what to do. There are no easy answers when, for example, in a partnership organization, many people with different perspectives need to be consulted. Setting direction can be problematic in these circumstances. It can often be seen that individual leaders are having difficulty with how to take up their authority in leadership roles without drawing on the "ghosts around the table" or past certainties of hierarchical leadership (Prins, 2002).

In this book, it is possible to see various ways in which the authors are assisting those in organizations to think and act more systemically. They are helping them not to retreat into the past, but to stay with ambiguity and open themselves to more meanings and, in so doing, to learn about and harness the system so that it can move forward more creatively with everyone on board. Given the enormous need for organizations and their leaders to develop new ways of thinking and working to meet current and future challenges, we hope other consultants will be inspired in their work by the inventive ways of working and new techniques presented in this book.

REFERENCES

Alberts, D. S., & Hayes, R. E. (2003). *Power to the Edge: Command and Control in the Information Age*. Washington, DC: US DoD Command and Control Research Program (available at http://dodccrp.org/publications/pdf/poweredge.pdf).

Andersen, T. (1987). The reflecting team: Dialogue and meta-dialogue in clinical work. *Family Process, 26*: 415–428.

Armstrong, D. (2004). Emotions in organizations: Disturbance or intelligence? In: C. Huffington, D. Armstrong, W. Halton, L. Hoyle, & J. Pooley (Eds.), *Working Below the Surface: The Emotional Life of Contemporary Organizations* (pp. 11–27). London: Karnac.

Armstrong, D. (2005). *Organization in the Mind*. London: Karnac.

Bachelard, G. (1969). *The Poetics of Space*. Boston, MA: Beacon.

Bakhtin, M. M. (1981). *The Dialogic Imagination: Four Essays*, ed. M. Holquist. Austin, TX: University of Texas.

Barnett, R. (2000). *Realising the University in an Age of Supercomplexity*. Buckingham: The Society for Research into Higher Education/Open University Press.

Bateson, G. (1972). *Steps to an Ecology of Mind*. New York: Chandler; Chicago, IL: Chicago University Press, 2000.

Batteau, P., Gosling, J., & Mintzberg, H. (2006). *The M, the B and the A*.

Exeter University Centre for Leadership Studies, Working Paper Series.

Becker, C., Chasin, L., Chasin, R., Herig, M., & Routh, S. (1995). From stuck debate to new conversations on controversial issues: A report from the Public Conversations Project. *Journal of Feminist Family Therapy, 71* (1/2): 143–163.

Belenky, M., Clinchy, B., Goldberger, N., & Tarule, J. (1997). *Women's Ways of Knowing.* New York: Basic Books.

Bell, J., & Huffington, C. (2008). Coaching for leadership development: A systems-psychodynamic approach. In K. Turnbull James & J. S. Collins, *Leadership Knowledge into Action.* Basingstoke: Palgrave Macmillan.

Bennis, W., & Thomas, R. (2002). *Geeks & Geezers.* Cambridge, MA: Harvard Business School Press.

Bertrando, P. (2007). *The Dialogical Therapist: Dialogue in Systemic Practice.* London: Karnac.

Bion, W. R. (1961). *Experiences in Groups.* London: Tavistock.

Bion, W. R. (1962). *Second Thoughts: Selected Papers on Psychoanalysis.* New York: Jason Aronson.

Block, P. (1981). *Flawless Consulting.* San Diego, CA: University Associates.

Bolden, R., Gosling, J., Marturano, A., & Dennison, P. (2003). *A Review of Leadership Theory and Competency Frameworks.* Exeter : University of Exeter Centre for Leadership Studies.

Booker, R. (2005). Integrated children's services: Implications for the profession. *Educational and Child Psychology, 22* (4): 127–142.

Boxer, P. J. (2004). Facing facts: What is the good of change? *Journal of Psycho-Social Studies, 3* (1, No. 4).

Boxer, P. J., & Eigen, C. (2005). Reflexive team supervision: Questioning "by whose authority". *Organisational and Social Dynamics, 5* (2): 257–279.

Boxer, P. J., & Palmer, B. (1994). Meeting the challenge of the case. In: R. Casemore et al. (Eds.), *What Makes Consultancy Work: Understanding the Dynamics* (pp. 358–371). London: South Bank University Press.

Boyatzis, R., & McKee, R. (2005). *Resonant Leadership.* Boston, MA: HBS Press.

Buber, M. (1970). *I and Thou.* New York: Scribner.

Buchanan, D. A. (2003). *Effective Organizations and Leadership Devel-*

opment: Trends and Issues. London: NHS Modernisation Agency Leadership Centre.

Burkitt, I. (1999). *Bodies of Thought.* London: Sage.

Burns, J. (1978). *Leadership.* New York: Harper & Row.

Burr, V. (1995). *An Introduction to Social Constructionism.* London: Routledge.

Burrell, D. (1997). *Pandemonium: Towards a Retro-Organization Theory.* London: Sage.

Campbell, D. (1995). *Learning Consultation: A Systemic Framework.* London: Karnac.

Campbell, D. (2000). *The Socially Constructed Organization.* London: Karnac.

Campbell, D., Coldicott, T., & Kinsella, K. (1994). *Systemic Work with Organizations: A New Model for Managers and Change Agents.* London: Karnac.

Campbell, D., Draper, R., & Huffington, C. (1991). *A Systemic Approach to Consultation.* London: Karnac.

Campbell, D., & Grønbæk, M. (2006). *Taking Positions in the Organization.* London: Karnac.

Case, P., & Gosling, J. (2007). Wisdom of the moment: Pre-modern perspectives on organizational action. *Social Epistemology, 21* (2): 87–111.

Cecchin, G. (1987). Hypothesizing, circularity and neutrality revisited: An invitation to curiosity. *Family Process, 26*: 405–413.

Cooper, A., & Dartington, T. (2004). The vanishing organization: Organizational containment in a networked world. In: C. Huffington, D. Armstrong, W. Halton, L. Hoyle, & J. Pooley (Eds.), *Working Below the Surface: The Emotional Life of Contemporary Organizations.* London: Karnac.

Cooperrider, D., & Avital, M. (2004), Introduction. In: *Advances in Appreciative Inquiry, Vol. 1: Constructive Discourse and Human Organization,* New York: Elsevier.

Cooperrider, D., & Whitney, D. (2001). *Appreciative Inquiry: A Positive Revolution in Change.* San Francisco, CA: Berrett-Koehler.

Coopey, J. (1995). The learning organization, power, politics and ideology. *Management Learning, 26* (2): 193–213.

Cronen, V., Johnson, K., & Lannaman, J. (1982). Paradoxes, double binds and reflexive loops: An alternative theoretical perspective. *Family Process, 21.*

Cronen, V., & Lang, W. P. (1994). Language and action: Wittgenstein and Dewey in the practice and therapy and consultation. *Human Systems: The Journal of Systemic Consultation and Management, 5* (1–2).

Cronen, V., & Pearce, W. B. (1985). Toward an explanation of how the Milan method works: An invitation to a systemic epistemology and the evolution of family systems. In: D. Campbell & R. Draper (Eds.), *Applications of Systemic Family Therapy: The Milan Approach.* London: Grune & Stratton.

Cronen, V., Pearce, W., & Tomm, K. (1985). A dialectical view of personal change. In: K. Gergen & K. Davis (Eds.), *The Social Construction of the Person.* New York: Springer-Verlag.

Dandelion, P. (2007). *An Introduction to Quakerism.* Cambridge: Cambridge University Press.

De Haan, E., & Burger, Y.(2005). *Coaching with Colleagues: An action Guide for One to One Learning.* London: Palgrave Macmillan.

Derrida, J. (1978). *Writing and Difference.* Chicago, IL: University of Chicago Press.

De Shazer, S. (1985). *Keys to Solution in Brief Therapy.* New York: W. W. Norton.

Dor, J. (1977). *Introduction to the Reading of Lacan.* New York: Jason Aronson.

Epston, D., White, M., & Murray, K. (1992). A proposal for re-authoring therapy. In: S. McNamee & K. J. Gergen (Eds.), *Therapy as Social Construction.* London: Sage (retrieved January 22, 2007, from http://home.mira.net/%7Ekmurray/psych/reauthor.htm).

Fielding, M. (2001). Learning organisation or learning community? A critique of Senge. *Reason in Practice, 1* (2): 17–29.

Foucault, M. (1980). *Power/Knowledge,* ed. C. Gordon. London: Harvester Wheatsheaf.

Frank, T. (2001). *One Market Under God.* New York: First Anchor Books.

Gabriel, Y. (2000). *Storytelling in Organisations: Facts, Fictions, Fantasies.* Oxford: Oxford University Press.

Gergen, K. J. (1994). *Realities and Relationships: Soundings in Social Construction.* Cambridge, MA: Harvard University Press.

Gergen, K. J. (1999). *An Invitation to Social Construction.* London: Sage.

Gladwell, M. (2000). *The Tipping Point: How Little Things Can Make a Big Difference.* New York: Little Brown.

Goldenberg, I., & Goldenberg, H. (1996). *Family Therapy: An Overview.* Belmont, CA: Brooks/Cole.

Grint, K. (2001). *The Arts of Leadership.* Oxford: Oxford University Press.

Grønbæk, M., & Pors, H. (2008). *VækstModellen—fra desillusion til begejstring* [The Growth Model—From Disillusion to Enthusiasm]. Frederikshavn, Ryslinge: Dafolo.

Grønbæk, M., Pors, H., Campbell, D., & Pors, J. G. (2008). *VækstModellen som ledelsesredskab* [The Growth Model in Management and Leadership]. Frederikshavn, Ryslinge: Dafolo.

Gwyn, D. (1984). *Apocalypse of the Word : The Life and Message of George Fox.* Richmond, IN: Friends United Press.

Hammond, S. A. (1996). *The Thin Book of Appreciative Inquiry.* Bend, OR: Thin Book Publishing.

Harré, R., & Langenhove, L. V. (1999). *Positioning Theory.* Oxford: Blackwell.

Harris, R. (2005). Teaching consultation skills: The manager as consultant. In: A. Southall (Ed.), *Consultation in Child and Adolescent Mental Health Services* (pp. 171–181). Oxford: Radcliffe.

Hart, V., Blattner, J., & Leipsic, S. (2001). Coaching vs. therapy: A perspective. *Consulting Psychology Journal: Practice & Research, 53* (4): 229–237.

Haslebo, G., & Nielsen, K. S. (2000). *Systems and Meaning: Consulting in Organizations.* London: Karnac.

Heifetz, R., & Laurie, D. (1997). The work of leadership. *Harvard Business Review* (January–February): 124–134.

Hieker, C., & Huffington, C. (2006). Reflexive questions in a coaching psychology context. *International Coaching Psychology Review, 1* (2): 46–56.

Hirschhorn, L. (1997). *The Primary Risk.* Philadelphia, PA: ISPSO Symposium.

Hodgart, A., & Mayson, S. W. (2006). *The Legal Business Guide to Law Firm Management.* London: Legalease.

Hoffman, L. (1981). *Foundations of Family Therapy: A Conceptual Framework for Systems Change.* New York: Basic Books.

Hoffman, L. (1993). *Exchanging Voices.* London: Karnac.

Huffington, C. (2006). A contextualised approach to coaching. In H. Brunning (Ed.), *Executive Coaching: Systems-Psychodynamic Approach.* London: Karnac.

Huffington, C., & Brunning, H. (1994). *Internal Consultancy in the Public Sector: Case Studies*. London: Karnac.

Huffington, C., James, K., & Armstrong, D. (2004). What is the emotional cost of distributed leadership? In: C. Huffington, D. Armstrong, W. Halton, L. Hoyle, & J. Pooley (Eds.), *Working Below the Surface: The Emotional Life of Contemporary Organizations* (pp. 67–82). London: Karnac.

Huffington, C., & Miller, S. (2008). Where angels and mere mortals fear to tread: Exploring "sibling" relations in the workplace. *Organisational and Social Dynamics, 8* (1): 18–37.

Jackson, D. (1957). The question of family homeostasis. *Psychiatry Quarterly Supplement, 31*: 79–99.

Keats, J. (1817). *The Letters of John Keats: A Selection*, ed. R. Gittings. Oxford: Oxford University Press, 1970.

Keeney, B. (1983). *Aesthetics of Change*. New York: Guilford Press.

Kilburg, R. R. (2002). *Executive Coaching: Developing Managerial Wisdom in a World of Chaos*. Washington, DC: American Psychological Society.

Kinsella, K. (2003). *How Do I Improve My Practice? Developing Pedagogy for the Education of Practitioners in Higher Education*. Diploma transfer paper, Centre for Action Research in Professional Practice, Bath University.

Klein, M. (1959). Our adult world and its roots in infancy. In: A. D. Colman & M. H. Geller (Eds.), *Group Relations Reader, Vol. 2*. Washington, DC: AK Rice.

Kolb, D. A. (1984). *Experiential Learning: Experience as the Source of Learning and Development*. Englewood Cliffs, NJ: Prentice-Hall.

Kouzes, J., & Posner, B. (2003). *The Leadership Challenge*. San Francisco, CA: Jossey-Bass.

Lacan, J. (1977). *The Four Fundamental Concepts of Psychoanalysis*. London: Hogarth Press. [Originally published in French by Éditions du Seuil, Paris, 1973.)

Lacan, J. (2006). *Écrits*. New York: W. W. Norton. [Originally published in French by Éditions du Seuil, Paris, 1966.]

Lakoff, G., & Johnson, M. (1999). *Philosophy of the Flesh: The Embodied Mind and Its Challenge to Western Thought*. New York: Basic Books.

Lawrence W. G. (2000). *Tongued with Fire: Groups in Experience*. London: Karnac.

Lawrence, W. G., Bain, A., & Gould, L. (1996). The fifth basic assumption. *Free Associations, 6* (1, No. 37): 28–55.

Lyotard, J.-F. (1984). *The Postmodern Condition: A Report on Knowledge.* Manchester: Manchester University Press.

Marshall, J. (2004). Living systemic thinking: Exploring quality in first person action research. *Action Research, 2* (3): 309–332.

Mason, B. (1993). Towards positions of safe uncertainty. *Human Systems: The Journal of Systemic Consultation and Management, 4*: 189–200.

Mason, J. (2002). *Researching Your Own Practice: The Discipline of Noticing.* London: Routledge Falmer.

Maturana, H. R., & Varela, F. V. (1980). *Autopoiesis and Cognition: The Realization of the Living. Boston Studies in the Philosophy of Science, Vol. 42.* Boston, MA: D. Reidel.

McCaughan, N., & Palmer, B. (1994). *Systems Thinking for Harassed Managers.* London: Karnac.

McKenna, E. (2000). *Business Psychology and Organisational Behaviour.* Hove: Psychology Press.

Menzies, I. (1959). The functioning of social systems as a defense against anxiety: A report on the study of a nursing service of a general hospital. *Human Relations, 13*: 95–121. Reprinted in I. Menzies Lyth, *Containing Anxiety in Institutions.* London: Free Association Books, 1988.

Menzies, I. (1960). Social systems as a defence against anxiety: An empirical study of the nursing service of a general hospital. In: E. Trist & H. Murray (Eds.), *The Social Engagement of Social Science, Vol. 1: The Socio-Psychological Perspective.* London: Free Association Books.

Metcalf, B. A., & Metcalf, J. A. (2005). Leadership: Time for a new direction. *Leadership, 1* (1): 51–71.

Miller, E. J., & Rice, A. K. (1967a). *Systems of Organization: Task and Sentient Systems and Their Boundary Control.* London: Tavistock Publications.

Miller, E. J., & Rice, A. K. (1967b). Task and sentient systems and their boundary controls. In: *The Social Engagement of Social Science, Vol. 1: The Socio-Psychological Perspective.* London: Free Association Books, 1990.

Minuchin, S. (1974). *Families and Family Therapy.* Cambridge, MA: Harvard University Press.

Minuchin, S., & Fishman, H. (1981). *Family Therapy Techniques*. Cambridge, MA: Harvard University Press.

Moore, R. (2000). *The Light In Their Consciences: Early Quakers in Britain 1646–1666*. University Park, PA: Pennsylvania State University Press.

Obholzer, A., & Miller, S. (Eds.) (2004). Leadership, followership, and facilitating the creative workplace. In: C. Huffington, D. Armstrong, W. Halton, L. Hoyle, & J. Pooley (Eds.), *Working Below the Surface: The Emotional Life of Contemporary Organizations*. London: Karnac.

Obholzer, A., & Roberts, V. Z. (Eds.) (1994). *The Unconscious at Work: Individual and Organizational Stress in the Human Services*. London: Routledge.

ODPM (2005). *Local Strategic Partnerships: Shaping Their Future*. London: Office of the Deputy Prime Minister.

Oliver, C. (1992). A focus on moral story making using co-ordinated management of meaning (CMM). *Human Systems: The Journal of Systemic Consultation and Management, 3*: 217–231.

Oliver, C. (1996). Systemic eloquence. *Human Systems: The Journal of Systemic Consultation and Management, 7* (4).

Oliver, C. (2005). *Reflexive Inquiry*. London: Karnac.

Oliver, C., Herasymowych, M., & Senko, H. (2003). *Complexity, Relationships and Strange Loops: A Reflexive Practice Guide*. Calgary, AB: MHA Institute.

Oliver, C., & Lang, S. (1994). Managing difficult people. *Managing in Local Government and Education* (November/December).

O'Neill, M. B. (2000). *Executive Coaching with Backbone & Heart: A Systems Approach to Engaging Leaders with Their Challenges*. San Francisco, CA: Jossey-Bass.

Palazzoli, M., Boscolo, L., Cecchin, G., & Prata, G. (1978). *Paradox and Counterparadox*. New York: Jason Aronson.

Pearce, W. B. (1994). *Interpersonal Communication: Making Social Worlds*. New York: Harper Collins.

Pearce, W. B., & Cronen, V. (1980). *Communication, Action, and Meaning: The Creation of Social Realities*. New York: Praeger.

Peltier, B. (2001). *The Psychology of Executive Coaching: Theory & Application*. New York: Taylor & Francis.

Penman, R. (1992). Good theory and good practice: An argument in process. *Communication Theory, 2* (3): 234–250.

Polanyi, M. (1983). *The Tacit Dimension.* Gloucester, MA: Peter Smith.

Prins, S. (2002). Helping and hindering dynamics in multi-party collaboration: Designing psychodynamic action research. In: D. Purdue & M. Stewart (Eds.), *Understanding Collaboration.* Bristol: University of the West of England Press.

Rayner, A. (2006). *Inclusionality.* Retrieved 30 December, 2006, from http://www.bath.ac.uk/~bssadmr/inclusionality

Rorty, R. (1980). *Philosophy and the Mirror of Nature.* Oxford: Blackwell.

Sampson, E. (1993). *Celebrating the Other.* London: Harvester Wheatsheaf.

Scharmer, O. (2006). *Theory U: Leading from the Future as It Emerges. Presencing as Social Technology of Freedom.* Retrieved 30 December, 2006, from http://www.ottoscharmer.com

Schön, D. (1983). *The Reflective Practitioner: How Professionals Think in Action.* New York: Basic Books.

Seikkula, J., & Arnkil, T. E. (2006). *Dialogical Meetings in Social Networks.* London: Karnac.

Selvini Palazzoli, M. (1986). *The Hidden Games of Organizations.* New York: Pantheon Books.

Senge, P. (1990). *The Fifth Discipline: The Art and Practice of the Learning Organization.* New York: Doubleday; London: Random House.

Shotter, J. (1993). *Conversational Realities: Constructing Life through Language.* London: Sage.

Stacey, R. (2003). *Complexity and Social Processes.* Hove: Brunner Routledge.

Starhawk (1986). *Truth or Dare: Encounters with Power, Authority, and Mystery.* New York: Harper & Row.

Tomm, K. (1987). Interventive interviewing: Part II. Reflexive questioning as a means to enable self-healing. *Family Process, 26:* 167–183.

Tomm, K. (1988). Interventive interviewing: Part III. Intending to ask lineal, circular, strategic and reflexive questions. *Family Process, 27:* 1–15.

Torbert, W. (2004). *Action Inquiry.* San Francisco, CA: Berret-Koehler.

Trevett, C. (1995). *Women and Quakerism in the 17th Century.* York: Ebor Press.

Turquet, P. M. (1974). Leadership: The individual and the group. In: G. S. Gibbard, J.-J. Harstrian, & R. D. Mann (Eds.), *Analysis of Groups.* San Francisco, CA: Jossey-Bass.

Van der Haar, D., & Hosking, D. M. (2004). Evaluating appreciative inquiry: A relational constructionist perspective. *Human Relations, 57* (8): 1017–1036.

Watzlawick, P., Weakland, C., & Fisch, R. (1974). *Change: Principles of Problem Formation and Problem Resolution.* New York: W. W. Norton.

Wenger, E. (1998). *Communities of Practice.* Cambridge: Cambridge University Press.

Western, S. (2005). *A Critical Analysis of Leadership: Overcoming Fundamentalist Tendencies.* PhD thesis, Lancaster University Management School.

Western, S. (2008). *Leadership: A Critical Text.* London: Sage.

White, M. (1997). *Narratives of Therapists' Lives.* Adelaide: Dulwich Centre.

Whitehead, J., & McNiff, J. (2006). *Action Research Living Theory.* London: Sage.

Whitmore, J. (1992). *Coaching for Performance: Growing People, Performance and Purpose.* London: Nicholas Brealey, 2002.

Wittgenstein, L. (1969). *On Certainty.* Oxford: Blackwell.

Wittgenstein, L. (1980). *Culture and Value.* Oxford: Blackwell.

Wood, M. (2005). The fallacy of misplaced leadership. *Journal of Management Studies, 42* (6): 1101.

Zuboff, S., & Maxmin, J. (2002). *The Support Economy.* New York: Viking.

INDEX

231